Flexible Thinker Guide to

Extreme
Career
Performance

Flexible Thinker Guide to

Extreme
Career
Performance

6 Steps to

- **Dramatically increase performance**

- **Career Entrepreneurship**

- **Resilience**

Sandra Boyd / Michael Rosenberg

*To Alex and Hope for all the joy and love
that you bring to those that love you.*

*To Rebecca and Hannah who never cease
to amaze me with their 'flexibility' and
constantly remind me of the importance
of liking what you do.*

Rosenberg, Michael / Boyd, Sandra
Extreme Performance

ISBN 0-9736361-0-6

Published by
Orange You Glad Inc.

Cover design by
Marc Jurman, Logomotion Graphics

Design production by
Fortunato Design Inc.

Printed and bound in Canada
Transcontinental Printing

CONTENTS

Forward: *What is Performance?*

In order to move forward, we must focus not on past grievances but on future visions.

—MICHAEL ROSENBERG

Eddie started out as a dedicated employee. Although he was a member of the union, he worked very hard as his job and tried to give an extra effort when he could. He did not particularly enjoy the work or think it was a great fit, but he realized he had a job to do and took pride in doing it. Eddie worked hard but there was never any recognition of his efforts. "Management was very controlling and thought very little of the job I did." commented Eddie. "Even a simple thank you would have gone a long way."

Finally Eddie gave up trying. He did not like his job, he was always fighting with management and he decided that he was going to do the minimal amount of work he could get away with. He no longer put in the extra effort and was ready to grieve any management decision that he did not like. He hated waking up in the morning and often times used his creativity not to produce more, but to actually find ways to do less. His only satisfaction was becoming an artist at 'getting away with things.'

Eddie had a secure job. He had been with the company for a long time and because of his union backing, he knew that there was no way that management could fire him. However, Eddie felt frustrated and unhappy. His strengths were not being utilized and everybody knew it. Although he was outgoing and people liked him, Eddie did not have a university degree so his options were limited in the organization. Management conflict and lack of recognition made the organization itself week. The only reason Eddie stayed in his job is because he truly believed that he needed the security of this dead-end job.

In his spare time, Eddie decided to explore becoming a real estate agent. He really enjoyed networking and selling, however, he was afraid to make it his full-time job. After all, there is no security in selling real estate and he had never had to sell before. He decided to stay with the job that he hated and pursue real estate 'one day.' Unfortunately, the stress from his job also affected his personal life. In addition to the frustrations of being stuck in a dead-end job, there were money problems. Everything was out of balance until, at the age of 37, Eddie had a heart attack at work.

Suddenly, change was forced on Eddie. He knew he could no longer take the stress of a job that he hated, so he decided to pursue a real estate career immediately. For many people, the idea of starting a new career where there is no guaranteed income would be stressful enough to send them to the hospital, but to Eddie it was invigorating. He connected with a strong real estate company where the broker mentored him. He was utilizing his skills and natural charisma to meet new people. He loved the challenge and was soon selling a steady stream of houses. In fact, by the time he had been selling real estate for four months, he was earning as much money as he would have made in a year at his safe unionized job. Eddie went from being ineffectual and a low performer, to being a significant asset and high performer.

Eddie's story illustrates two points: anyone can be a high performer or low performer—it depends on the job that you have and, it takes a personal and physical toll when your talents are not being utilized effectively.

Eighty-five percent of a company's assets walk out the door every day. Employees are the ultimate reason for the success or failure of many businesses. A core function of human resource departments can be summarized in two words—maximizing performance. How a human resource department tackles that challenge can mean the difference between it being integral to the organization, or a liability.

The only reason that organizations exist is to solve problems. For instance, the problem of getting from one place to another is solved by the use of cars, buses, planes, etc. Likewise, each job only exists to solve problems. If there were no problems, there would be no jobs. Since the only reason that organizations exist is to let their individual employees solve problems for their clients, it stands to reason that the entire purpose of the human resource department is to maximize the performance of the organization's people. An organization's best friend and worst enemy might be the same person, depending on who is utilized to solve what problem. The ability to effectively solve problems is what is at the heart of performance.

As Eddie's story demonstrates, performance is tied to three things—the strength of the organization/team, the individual's job/career, and a balanced personal life. When you have the right job and a balanced personal life but the organization falters, you have unemployment. When you have a balanced personal life and the organization is strong but you are in the wrong job, you have ineffectiveness. Finally, when you have the right job in a strong organization but no personal life, you are prone to burnout and sickness.

What is Extreme Career Performance?

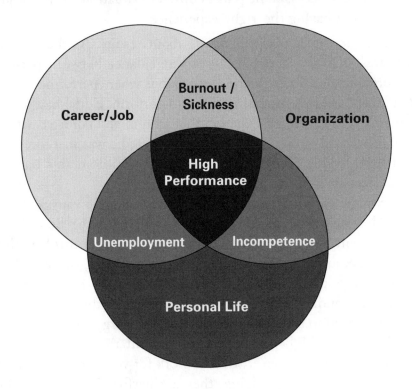

High performance is not about:

- **Age.** You can be a high performer at any age.
- **Education.** There are high performers who have dropped out of high school and low performers with PhDs.
- **Background/Gender/Language.** Whether you are a man or a woman, from Santiago or San Francisco, performance is about results.
- **Physical strength.** Jim Abbott pitched a no-hitter for the California Angels with just one arm. Everybody has strengths, and performance is about utilizing your strengths to their greatest benefit.
- **Experience.** You can have a lot of experience in doing things poorly or apply a different outlook to a problem to create a solution. We all have experiences in our lives that we can access to help us in different situations. It is not just about having the 'right' experience.

Extreme career performance is about results. As the diagram indicates, it is also about balance. The balance between personal life, organizational health and career/job is where performance lies. You must have this balance in order to perform. Eddie had to take control of his career, find the job that fit him and connect with an established and strong realty company where he was mentored and find time for his family and personal life. Without this balance, Eddie became sick and ineffective.

Extreme career performance lies with you. It is your responsibility because you are the one who will reap the benefits of achievement the most. High performers are in control of their careers. Because they are in the right job and being utilized fully, they are producing for the organization and are happy in their careers. By finding time for their personal lives, they get the support they need to constantly replenish their energy so that they can continue to be high performers throughout their working lives. High performers are never without work for very long. Even when facing lay-offs or downsizing, they are performing because they have the tools to take their accomplishments and market them into better opportunities. Their balance leads them to 'win-win' in its truest sense.

How do you achieve high performance in your own career and life? It all starts with your mindset. As we go through this book, our goal is to give you the tools to perform in your career even when you are facing difficulties. It is fundamentally up to you. The bad news is that the days of a job for life when a paternalistic organization managed your career and handed you a balanced life on a silver platter are gone. The good news is that the opportunities open to you are endless. All you need are the tools to access them.

There is a very simple definition for flexibility. It is having options. Simply put, the more options you have, the more flexible you can be. The purpose of this book is to give you the tools you need to create options so that you will never again be afraid of losing your job or losing control of something as important as your career. This book and these tools will empower you to control your career, whatever the external circumstances are that surround you.

For me, this publication is a natural outgrowth of *The Flexible Thinker*® program and book. When I met Sandra, the co-author of this book, we compared her work in employment with my work in flexibility and leadership, and both realized that now more than ever, people need to take control of their professional lives.

That is why this book is fundamentally about empowerment. You can no longer depend on a person or organization to be responsible for your career. You need to have the tools to take control of your career yourself.

Chapter One:

The Evolution of Employment

*The definition of insanity is doing the same thing
over and over again and expecting a different result.*

—BENJAMIN FRANKLIN

UNDERSTANDING THE 21ST CENTURY JOB MARKET

Mike's Story

My favourite story about Gandhi goes something like this. A woman went to Gandhi with her son and asked him to tell the boy to stop eating candy. Gandhi told the woman to go away and come back a week later. The woman did as she was told and came back to Gandhi, son in tow. Gandhi then looked at the young boy and told him to stop eating candy. The woman looked at him, very puzzled, and asked Gandhi why she had to wait a week for him to say something so simple to her son. "Because," Gandhi replied, "a week ago I was eating candy."

There are so many self-help books with wonderful pearls of wisdom out there. Many organizations are also offering great advice and training in a whole host of skill development and career management courses. Yet, the key question should always be, 'Do these people walk their talk?' Sandra and I believe it is very important to share our own personal stories. That is why you will find that the tools that we talk about in this book did not come from academic research; we applied them ourselves to succeed in our own careers.

My story goes back to more than 10 years ago. It was winter and the bleakness of the weather was only surpassed by the bleakness I felt inside. I was at a dead end. "For the first time since I have known you, I am scared," my wife told me. "You have no ideas about what to do."

To be honest, at that moment I had given up. My dreams were disappearing and I had no idea what to do next. I always wanted to be a screenwriter/playwright. The show that I had produced, although it generated terrific reviews, left my wife and I near bankruptcy. I was in desperate shape. My wife was working seven days a week to keep us afloat financially and we were on the verge of losing our house. The job market was very tight and every idea I had seemed to blow up in my face. My wife was right; I had run out of ideas.

All I wanted was a job, any job. I no longer had the luxury to think about a career. I was going for interviews for secretarial jobs, anything that I could find. I finally landed a job as a secretary for a large investment house. I was happy to be contributing, but I was not an easy person to be around at that point in my life. I hated my job and the commute back and forth. I hated the regimented and stiff environment that stifled any creativity I still had left. Still, I was determined to make it work. I always worked very hard and had a good reputation as a person who could solve problems.

One day, my boss was faced with a difficult problem. He had to present a plan to cut $12 million from his budget within two weeks. I heard about this and went to him with a simple plan that I estimated would save the company around $18 million. His response was, "You're not a manager. Only the managers come up with the ideas around here." Needless to say, I learned more about management in those five minutes than an M.B.A. does in three years. I immediately decided that I needed to get out of there. At that moment, my body may have been there, but my brain was miles away.

When I started to look around, I felt a lot of fear. After all, I had a family to support and had already lost a lot of money producing a play I wrote. Adding to my fear were the negative tapes playing in the back of my head that kept asking me, "Who do you think you are?" It was then that I knew that if I was ever going to have a real career, something that I could enjoy and be proud of, I had to start by changing my thinking.

That is where I got the idea to redefine who I was and how I should manage my career. I realized that, at the end of the day, I really only worked for myself and that that was the direction I wanted to go in. My wife and mother thought that I should teach and, I built on their idea. I knew that I wanted to do something worthwhile in my life and I was very motivated. The only problem was that I did not want to go back to school to get my teaching certificate and really had no desire to teach elementary or high school.

I started to network and developed a relationship with the dean of one of the community colleges who knew about my improvisation and theatre work. He offered me a part-time job teaching improvisation to radio and television students. Through this work, I met other people who were doing corporate training. When they saw my work, they suggested that I do creativity/innovation training using the tools that I had developed while running a business and performing. The rest, as they say, is history. I wrote my first book, *The Flexible Thinker®: A Guide to Creative Wealth*, and I have never looked back since.

Sandra's Story

At the ripe old age of 17, my son Sean was born. From that moment, I knew that my life would present challenges and roadblocks as I moved from one stage to the next. I also knew that I was the one responsible for the outcome of my life. Even at 17, I realized that I must be accountable and had to take control of the direction that I was heading.

My first decision was to go back to high school when my son was only six months old. I will always be grateful, for I was lucky to have the encouragement and support of my parents throughout the years. After graduating, I went to the Eaton Centre in Toronto and started to apply for positions in stores. After a few hours of walking the mall, I was finally hired by a card and gift store. Little did I know just how hard I would have to work for very little money. I spent a year acquiring customer service skills until I decided that I needed to find a position that would pay more money and inject some 'glamour' into my life.

I landed a position with a well-known women's clothing store. The position paid a minimum hourly wage plus commission for everything I sold. However, I was up against seasoned hustlers and spent the first three months of my new job trying not to step on any toes. During those three months I lost more sales to my competitive colleagues than I made extra money.

It was tough, and they did not make it easy. I learned to respect and admire these amazing women who make their careers in women's fashion. After they realized I was there to stay and was not going to give up, the women started to take pity on me and I became their pet project.

They taught me the art of approaching a potential customer as she walked into the store and how to give the nod to every other salesperson to show that the customer was mine. I learned how to recognize a buyer from a time waster, and how to double a sale by adding earrings and scarves to every outfit I sold. I also learned techniques to build an exclusive clientele by tracking phone numbers, dress sizes and color and style preferences for preferred customers and then phoning these customers when new merchandise came into the store. I finally started making sales and was rewarded with commission cheques every month. For one full year I worked hard to become a relaxed and natural salesperson and combined that skill set with the outstanding customer service skills I already had under my belt.

It was still not enough. I knew that if I was to provide my son with a better life I needed a better paying job. So, I invested the huge sum of $700 on a secretarial administrative course, which I paid off from my weekly paycheque. It would take one year of evenings and weekends to earn my secretarial diploma.

Armed with my diploma, I started to look for work and was thrilled to land a job as a receptionist/secretary at a small but growing company that built exhibits for trade shows. Unfortunately, the pay was not as much as I was making as a sales clerk, so I continued to work part-time at the store and took the position with the exhibit company for the experience.

It soon became painfully clear that I was not the best typist in the world and that my spelling (there was no spell-check then) left a lot to be desired. However, the industry was deadline driven and I had the ability to calm customers and defuse situations between the salespeople who brought in the work, the artists who designed the exhibits and the tradespeople who built the finished product. I was also able to gently push the installers to get the job completed on time. My saving grace was that I also had the skill to collect on old debts. When the president of the company discovered this, he decided that my talents would be better served running the office, instead of typing letters. He gave me a raise which allowed me to quit my part-time position at the store.

After two years as the office manager I approached the president and asked him if I could move into sales. He laughed and immediately denied my request. I was furious, and he tried to calm me down by explaining that I was too nice of a young lady to be a salesperson in the exhibit industry. After all, he explained, there was only one woman in the industry and she was tough as nails. The president's final words to me on the subject were, "Sandra there is no way in hell you could be successful or survive as a sales rep in this industry. Stick to what you are good at!" Then he offered me a raise. I still quit two months later.

For the next year and a half I became a temp moving from one company to the next, gaining skills while eliminating careers such as marketing, engineering and anything to do with the sciences. My experiences helped me understand clearly what I did not want to do—it was eye-opening. I would quickly change my mind about companies I had dreamed of working for when I discovered that I was not suited to their environments or culture. Although being a temp never helped define what I wanted to do, it did give me a long list of things I did not want to do. When trying to make an informed decision about the direction your life is going in, this can be just as important.

At one of the services I worked for, I decided to ask my contact if she thought I would be a good fit for that industry. She was surprised by my interest and suggested that I apply for a position that was available in their downtown office. I jumped at the chance and went to meet with the branch manager.

I landed the position and started my new job three weeks later. It was the start of a 15-year career in the staffing industry. I had finally found my home—a place where I knew I belonged. I loved the industry, the challenge of the job, the learning curve and helping people. I really enjoyed the adrenaline rush when I placed a person in a new position and built the relationship with the client. Finally, I was making the money I needed to support my son and build my life.

Three years into my new career, I opened my own agency with my partner Lorraine in the prestigious Royal Bank Plaza in downtown Toronto. Over the next two years, business grew so that we were able to hire staff. However, in our third year everything fell apart. The market hit bottom in 1989 and business died. We had to lay off our staff and finally had to walk away from the business we loved. Lorraine and I lost everything, including ourselves for a period of time.

I was devastated and did not know what I was going to do with my life. How could I start over? Losing that business was like losing a piece of myself. It was tied into my self-worth. It was who I was! I had lost every dime I had ever made and more. For months I stayed at home, watched *Oprah* and made casseroles. I did not want to face the world or my future.

The market was so horrible that I applied for anything and everything as long as it was not in the staffing industry. I could not bear to go back and work for someone else in an industry I felt I had failed in. So, I tried selling wedding packages, children's clothing and exhibits for trade shows for a friend. I designed a child's leash with a puppy on the wrist to keep kids safe when they went out with their parents and even applied for a position selling funeral packages. In the end, however, I could not do it. I had lost my way and my focus.

With my husband's support and help I finally went back to the staffing industry with the sole intention of earning money. That was when I found a position with Manpower. It was the break that finally helped me to get back on the career track and regain my confidence. There, I met my friend Stacy, my mentor and friend Deborah and the senior management team of Mary, Susan and Judi. They truly supported my growth and allowed me individual opportunities. I owe so much to them and to the other wonderful and supportive women that I had the pleasure of working with every day.

I worked at Manpower for five years until I decided to write my first book, *The Hidden Job Market* (McGraw-Hill, 1998). Writing that book changed my life and gave me the confidence to move into yet another industry—outplacement. I quit my corporate job and started a small consulting business where I wrote articles, authored and facilitated workshops and coached individuals. I was even invited to speak at an authors' Chapters event organized and hosted by another writer, Michael Rosenberg. For more than two years Michael and I would periodically network until finally over coffee we decided to combine our expertise to write this book.

My career has not traveled the traditional path. There have been many detours and potholes along the way. In spite of that, I would not change it. Over the years I have been back to school to retool and update my skills a dozen or more times. The journey has been filled with excitement and surprises and has been rich with experiences that have all led to this book.

The Evolution of Employment

Joanne is frozen with fear. Her stomach is in knots waiting for the 'next cut.' "I am swimming in stress," she confesses.

Like many other people in today's job market, Joanne feels the dual conflict of spending time with her family and putting in the hours she needs to keep up with the workload at the office. "On a daily basis I find myself discussing the next cut with my co-workers—who will who will keep their positions and who will be downsized and when that day will come. The rumor mill has been in overdrive these last few weeks. It's really hard to be fired up and creative about my job if I am going to be walked out the door in the near future."

Joanne has worked in the finance department for a large telecommunications company for the past five years and has already survived three cuts. Like many of her co-workers, she has not prepared for what will eventually happen—the loss of her own job.

We followed up with Joanne 10 months later and she told us that the rumour mill was still alive and well. From all accounts, her boss might even lose her job due to downsizing. We asked Joanne if she had taken our advice and started any kind of career management activities to prepare herself for losing her job, she again told us that she was too busy at work to think of looking for another job.

Joanne is not alone with her fear and the stress it can create. Many of the employees that survive corporate downsizing feel grateful at first that they still have a job, but after their colleagues have left, they soon notice an increase in hours, workloads and pressure. The epidemic is worldwide. In Canada, for instance, more than one in three people experience a high level of work-life conflict, suffering depression, stress and burnout. In addition, workplace violence and absenteeism are up and productivity is down.

Although facts, statistics and demographics are boring to the majority of people, they also confirm that we are not alone feeling the way that we do about work. Most people that we work with believe they are stressed out. They often blame themselves for not being able to effectively balance work and personal life. Take a moment to review the facts and stats that are part of the 21st century workplace and how they are affecting employers and employees around the world.

- More than one in three people experience a high level of work-life conflict, suffering depression, stress and burnout.

- The average work week is now between 48 to 49 hours, whereas 20 years ago people were working 41 hours per week.

- Workplace violence is up, absenteeism is up, productivity is down.

- Employee surveys state that the average American takes about 9 days of vacation a year, the average Canadian takes an average of only 8.72 days per year while the average European takes 30 days per year.

- Nine percent of North American employees limit themselves to a day or two off in vacation time per year instead of taking time off consecutively.

- Absenteeism because of work-life conflict costs organizations an estimated $2.77 billion in output annually in Canada alone.

A conservative average on how many times a businessperson must shift concepts, or shift their focus of attention is at least seven to eight times an hour. This constant changing of focus is a very real creator of stress. Does it simply mean people are 'stressed out'? The answer is that this has a real effect on the bottom line. For instance, consider these worldwide figures:

- Organizational change causes productive work to drop from 4.8 hours per day to 1.2 hours per day, a loss of 75 percent.
- In Canada, at least $12 billion is spent annually on trackable stress-related costs.
- Karoshi—dying at your desk—is considered a national health crisis in Japan, affecting tens of thousands each year.
- Sixty-one percent of people surveyed in the U.S., U.K., Ireland, Germany, Singapore and Hong Kong, believe information overload is present in their workplace, with 80 percent predicting that the situation will worsen.
- Three 10-year studies concluded that emotional stress was more predictive of death from cancer and cardiovascular disease than smoking; people who were unable to effectively manage their stress had a 40 percent higher death rate than more emotionally managed individuals.

What Does This Mean to You?

Why are you working to the point of burnout? Are you placing loyalty to the company above loyalty to yourself and your family? Take a moment. Close your eyes. Now, imagine that you are at your funeral. What did you leave behind?

The workplace started a complete evolution of employment in the 1980's when downsizing for profit became a way of life for the corporate world. You need to take charge by managing your career—whether you work for somebody else or yourself. You have to be prepared at all times for changes in the economy and the job market. You can do this easily and effortlessly if you understand your role in the workplace and acknowledge that you have a responsibility to manage your career. This means that you should stop depending on the corporation to decide your future. You have the power to change your situation.

The fact that you are reading this book states you now believe that you are solely responsible for your career and its future. The old rules no longer apply. The key to being able to manage your own career is to be adaptable. Your success will depend on how flexible you can be in changing circumstances. That is why we have written this book. The measurement of the success of your working life is your ability to be a 'flexible thinker.' Times are changing rapidly. It is like a great big wave and you now have two choices— get swallowed up by the wave and drown, or get the surfboard you need to ride the wave.

How has the Workplace Changed?

Right on the corner of Dupont and Christie in Toronto is where Planters Peanuts was located for as long as I could remember. Out of those windows every year my brother, sister and I watched the Santa Claus parade go by. After the parade was over, Santa made a special stop at the peanut factory to bring presents to all the children of the employees. They were the same children, the same employees every year of my childhood. I remember all the wonderful ladies who my father worked with every day for over 25 years coming over to our table to discuss how big my brother, sister and I had grown over the year. My father ended up as the production supervisor at Planters after beginning there as a floor sweeper.

When I got older, my parents would take me to the adults' Christmas party and the same ladies would again exclaim over how I had grown. We never socialized with most of these people, but they would send cards to our house for Christmas, birthdays, births and deaths, and my mother would do the same in return. We considered them friends. The years went by and the mergers and takeovers started to affect many companies including Planters Peanuts until finally, after a number of mergers and sales, a large multinational bought my dad's company.

Yes, I said my dad's company. My dad did not just *work* at Planters he *lived* for Planters. My mother said it was his mistress. He was dedicated, loyal and missed countless dinners and special family occasions on account of his company. He loved his job and the people he worked with. After years of devoted service, there was no doubt that a little piece of the company belonged to my father. But as with so many things, the time had come to take over and change what once was. For Planters, this meant moving from Dupont and Christie to Smiths Falls, Ontario, four hours away.

We all held our breath. Would my dad be offered a job, or a package? The offer of relocation came, and the family was separated for the first time—only by a few hours, but it was an adjustment for all. My dad was up for the challenge and excited. My mother believed that a much more cynical plot was unfolding. Intuition told her that the new owners would learn everything about the peanut business and drop the old management team as soon as they had gained the required knowledge. So, my mom's advice to my dad was, "Take your time teaching them about the peanut business."

Maybe mom was right, or maybe she simply had an overactive imagination, but within seven years most of the old staff were gone. One week before my sister's wedding, dad was called into an office, handed his belongings and, in the company of a transition consultant, escorted to the front door.

As a consultant who specialized in career transition I know this is the proper way to sever a working relationship with a long-term employee, especially during a downsizing. As a daughter, it broke my heart to think my father gave his heart and a good part of his life to a company that repaid him in such a callous manner.

When my dad was given the 'golden handshake,' it affected more than just him, it hurt the whole family and our hearts ached as we watched him struggle through an experience he could only consider a personal humiliation. It also hurt financially as my father was over 50 but not yet ready to retire. He has never really talked about it, but I know by the look in his eyes that he lost more than just his job that day.

My father's advice to me as I was going off to look for my first job was to get my foot in the door of a stable company where I could climb the corporate ladder and get a gold watch and pension at the end of my 25 or so years of employment with that one company. That is no longer the reality of individuals in the workplace. We can no longer count on companies for our pensions, training and opportunity to climb the corporate ladder. In many cases, company benefits are no longer even part and parcel of the company contract that we once held with our employers.

In 1956 William H. Whyte Jr., an editor at *Fortune*, wrote the *Organization Man*. The book was on the best-seller list for seven months and on corporate and college reading lists for several decades. It placed the corporation at the core of our belief system. If we were loyal to the organization, the organization would be loyal to us. The company was the centre of our very existence.

The company decided when and if we could make more money, climb the corporate ladder to the next position, and even if we were best suited to remain in one position for our career lifetime. In most cases, the belief of career acceleration was based on tenure and not on ability. The companies of the 20th century were all-knowing and set social ethics. They were the masters, and employees followed to ensure a spot in a so-called secure company.

Prior to the *Organization Man* and the industrial revolution, we were free agents, entrepreneurs and small business owners. We were farmers, shopkeepers, blacksmiths, doctors, lawyers, bakers and candlestick makers. We had to arrange our own retirement and look after each other during sickness and crisis.

At the beginning of this chapter, we used the quote, "The definition of insanity is doing the same thing over and over again and expecting different results." We chose it because it is our belief that it is not good enough to change a few habits and apply some new tools. You have to look at the very core of your belief system to rebuild and reposition yourself for the next stage of your career.

Exercise

Beliefs in the Workplace and the Role of Loyalty

Take the time to reflect and answer each of these questions.

1   What is the first piece of advice your parents gave you when you started your career?

2   How has that belief changed since you began your career?

3   What do you now believe to be true about corporations and executives in today's workplace?

4   Moving forward, what three expectations do you have of an employer/corporation?

5   What three expectations do you think an employer/corporation has of you as an employee?

6   Name three things you regret doing/not doing for your last employer/corporation?

7   What are you willing to do to be successful in the workplace?

8   What are you no longer willing to do to be successful in the workplace?

9   What is the one thing you will do differently as an employee in your next position?

When we ask participants in our workshops to do this exercise, it never ceases to amaze us that at least half of the group will have 'aha moments.' For instance, after completing this exercise, Laura shared with the group that from the start of her career her highly successful father told her that if you are not number one in what you do, you should pack it in and go home because you have lost.

At that moment, in front of 20 other people, she broke down and told us that for her whole life she has felt like a failure and she just discovered the reason why. Laura has owned two businesses, has been involved in countless ventures and was also recognized as 'Women of the Year' by her community. When we first met her we were so impressed by her energy and experiences that we wanted her to work with us, yet she had spent her whole career believing that she was a failure.

Is Employer/Employee Loyalty Dead?

What's old is new. According to Daniel H. Pink, author of *Free Agent Nation*, we are now in a work culture in which fewer than one in ten North Americans work for a Fortune 500 company. The largest private employer in the U.S. in 2002 was not Detroit's General Motors or Ford, or even Seattle's Microsoft or Amazon.com, but Milwaukee's Manpower Inc.

According to a January 2004 *Toronto Star* article written by Vera N. Held, employees are increasingly detaching from the job as a result of being overwhelmed by work. The same article cited work/life balance—all but ignored by employers because of crisis after crisis (SARS, Mad Cow disease, blackout, etc.) in 2003—as one of the biggest concerns for employees that year. Uncertainty in the workplace has had a direct effect on how we view the corporations we work for.

Many of us have replaced loyalty with cynicism and view corporations and their executives suspiciously. Who could blame us? We just have to look at companies like Enron, Nortel and Tyco to understand why many employees now have the perception that they are being taken advantage of, seriously lied to, cheated out of money and can no longer trust corporations.

I believe that for our own sanity we need to stop focusing on the corporation and start focusing on what we believe is true for our own individual careers. Downsizing is now part of our work culture and being prepared for that event throughout our careers is the sole responsibility of the individual, not the corporation. As employees, we can no longer give our emotional energy away to corporations, but should instead focus on a complete shift in our beliefs about loyalty.

In today's workplace, loyalty is not obsolete it is just different. Instead of being loyal to the company as a whole, we can now place our loyalty on the project, the team and management for the period of time we are working on that project. According to Statistics Canada, the average job lasts 2.5 years, so as employees we will be constantly shifting our loyalty from project to project even in a so-called secure, full-time position. We do not have to throw loyalty out the window, we just need to change where we focus it.

Loyalty is an important gift that we give to our families, friends, associations, political parties, countries, religions and so many other aspects of our lives. Without the human loyalty factor, we would feel a sense of disconnection. Imagine the workplace where everyone has consciously decided to go to work and just put in time. There is actually a phrase for this. *Ghosting* means that physically we are there, but mentally and emotionally we have left the building.

It is understandable that we have become disillusioned by the corporate world and the changes that have occurred over the last 20 years. However, it is time for us to begin to reposition our careers and begin the journey that allows each of us to foster an entrepreneurial spirit and take control of our own careers.

Chapter Two:

The '*Me Inc.*' Attitude

Perfect freedom is reserved for the man
who lives by his own work and in that work
does what he wants to do.

—ROBIN GEORGE COLLINGWOOD

There is no word to describe Gavin other than genius. An advanced degree from Oxford, number one law school graduate student in the country and a position clerking for a Supreme Court justice are just the beginning of his resumé. After being called to the bar, he was one of the most sought-after lawyers in the country. The most prestigious law firms recruited him and finally, after fielding a number of lucrative offers, he chose an international law firm with a stellar reputation.

"I love the law and had this idea that that would be enough since I was being employed in the pursuit of the law. Boy, was I wrong."

Things went bad for Gavin almost immediately. He doesn't suffer fools gladly and did not hesitate to correct senior partners. He also found it difficult to communicate clearly with clients. "Gavin is a brilliant jurist," commented one of the partners, "but that is not what pays the bills here."

Gavin soon found himself on the outs and was passed over for partnership. Eventually, he got the message and found himself another job at a different law firm. The same thing happened there and he was eventually asked to leave. Now Gavin, the brilliant lawyer who was on the sure track to become a judge, was forced to work as a sole practitioner.

"I was totally unprepared for this," Gavin confesses. Now he had to do all of the things that university never prepared him for in order to succeed. "I had to find clients, market myself, collect bills and bite my tongue. It took a real toll on me. I discovered that many times knowing the law is secondary to understanding people. Nobody ever told me that I would have to become an entrepreneur."

Gavin learned a difficult lesson. Hard skills will get you the job, but it is the 'soft' skills—communication, leadership, flexibility and presentation skills—that will allow you to keep the job and thrive in it. He also learned that everybody has to be an entrepreneur today. The idea of a lawyer or an MBA being unemployed was unheard of, even a few years ago. Yet today, even post-graduate degrees are no longer guarantees for jobs.

Flexible Thinker Tool #1

Orange

Go to the refrigerator and find yourself an orange. Examine it carefully.

Now, let us tell you a story about oranges. As of this second they have been found to be bad for your health. Even the name 'Orange' is now synonymous with death and destruction. If you don't believe that this can happen in the real world, I have one very simple example for you—'British beef.' Remember, something that was thought to be good for you one minute, can be capable of melting your brain the next.

The problem is this. You have 150,000 crates of oranges that you must sell somehow. There is only one rule. You can no longer use oranges as food or drink in any form. That means you cannot take the oranges and make them into orange juice, marmalade, soufflés or sherbet.

Now, pick up the orange and explore it. What else can you use it for? Come up with 10 different names and uses for the object. Let's get you started. You can call it a 'ball' and use it to play a game of catch. You could also call it compost and use it to fertilize your garden. These are some obvious names and uses like 'soap' and it 'can be used to wash your hands'. Now come up with 10 on your own. Write them on a piece of paper. Don't be afraid to be wild. Make up crazy names and uses. This is the time to do that. Call it a wazemo and make up a different use!

Your first tool—ORANGE
Orange means to
Redefine* and *Think Three-dimensionally

At one workshop, a participant told us that when he first graduated he sent out six resumés and got four job offers. He had an MBA, a CPA and was also a CFA (certified financial analyst). When he was downsized, he thought that it would be a perfect opportunity to take a year off and explore other options. "What I found is that all of a sudden I couldn't simply send out a few resumés and get a bunch of responses," sighs Tom. "I didn't know what to do. The idea of career management was so foreign to me. Back home, the CEO personally called me to offer me a job and now I have to go through layers and wait for answers. I looked and could find no central authority with specific tools on how to deal with this. I was really lost."

How are you looking at the orange? Are you looking at it on a table in front of you or holding it in your hand across from your eye? Are you simply imagining the orange in your head and looking at it directly across from you? If so, you are viewing the orange from a two-dimensional angle. Now take it and put it on the top of your head. What other ideas do you have for the orange? Now move it to your ear, on the floor, on your left breast, on your nose. What other ideas can you develop?

Apply this exercise to your career and your challenges. Are you stuck looking at them two-dimensionally?

Think about the power of what you have just done. People have looked at oranges the same way for 5,000 years! What do you do with an orange? You peel it and eat it or you squeeze the juice out of it and drink it. That is what your parents did and their parents before them and their parents before them, etc. Yet, within the span of a few minutes, you were able to create a series of options with that object that do not include the obvious. What is an orange? It is nothing but an everyday object that you have looked at a thousand times and never given much thought. After all, what can you do with an orange besides eating and drinking it?!? If you can create options with an orange, then you can do the same with yourself, your challenges and, most of all, your career.

How Does the Orange Apply to Your Career?

What happened to how you looked at the orange when you started giving it new names and uses? All of a sudden, instead of looking at the object as you had seen it for years, it started to look different. Instead of seeing problems, you saw opportunities.

Patricia wanted new shelves for her research department. The old shelves that she had were ugly and falling apart. "It was depressing looking at them every day," she sighed. "Because this was a research area and we had to build the shelves to a certain code and they had to be sterile, I discovered the cost would be $20,000. I then went to my director and told him that I needed $20,000 for new shelves. He told me, 'Sorry, it's not in the budget.' So I went back to him again and said I REALLY need new shelves and he said we REALLY don't have it in the budget. It was like that quote about insanity—doing the same thing over and over again and expecting a different result."

As we went through the orange exercise, she started *redefining* what she was asking from her director. Instead of asking for 'new shelves', she thought about the old ones and redefined it as a 'health and safety' concern. After all, the old shelves were starting to fall apart and they could hurt somebody if they collapsed at the wrong time or fell down.

After the course, she went back to her director and asked if there was room in the budget to resolve a potential health and safety concern. "Yes, there is," he indicated. "Otherwise we may end up facing a lawsuit." She told him she needed $20,000 to solve it and that afternoon she got the budget approval. The new shelves we installed by the end of the week.

When you redefine, you broaden your options. By 'orangeing' the situation, Patricia was able to find an answer to her problem. It is the same with managing your career. Because the only constant in employment today is change, you need to constantly redefine yourself and your skills. Even as you make your career plans, circumstances change and you may find that jobs that were 'hot' one day are a dime-a-dozen the next. By taking your skills and redefining them, you can adapt to the market and create options for yourself. That is the difference between managing your career and always having to react to the next layoff or downsizing.

NASA had a 'meet an astronaut' event at their Cape Kennedy-facility in Florida. Scott Carpenter, the famed Apollo astronaut who was featured in such books as *The Right Stuff* talked about what it was like preparing and going to space. He then took a few moments to answer questions from the audience. One person specifically asked him how he changed when he went to space. He talked for a few moments about physical changes to the body and bone density, but it was what he said about emotional changes that was really interesting.

"Once you have seen the Earth from that viewpoint," he commented, "you never look at the Earth the same way again. Not only do you never see the Earth the same way again, you never see anything the same way again—your spouse, your co-workers, your kids, your neighbors, your job, even your dog. Your entire perspective changes."

It is the same with an orange. Now, since most of us will never be fortunate enough to fly to outer space, we can throw the orange and come up with a number of different uses. Once we do that, we will never look at an orange the same way again. Once we have changed our perspective, we will never see things in the same way again.

You Have Now Been 'Oranged'

Let's apply this tool specifically to your career. You have now been redefined as the president and CEO of a new company. This company is called *Me Inc.* and it has a very important product that is essential for any business to be successful. It is a product that is just as vital for an organization when times are good, as it is when times are bad. It is something that changes to meet its customers' demands. What is that product? That product is YOU!

Even though the product is you, you are not the product! What does that mean? It means that even though you are a vital service, you may not be the right product for everybody. For instance, if you need something to clean your clothes, you will not buy a toaster. It is the wrong product to meet that need. Do you think that the manufacturer of the toaster takes it personally that you did not buy their product at that specific time? Also, let's say that there are a number of new toasters that are built well, deliver a number of services and have been recommended by others. Which toaster do you think you are likely to buy when you need to find an answer to how you can heat your bread? What if the market shifts and people are no longer eating bread but bagels and your toaster cannot fit a bagel but somebody else's can? Which toaster do you think people will buy?

As the president and CEO of *Me Inc.*, you now have to think like a corporate executive who has a product to sell. What does your product do?

- No matter what you think you do for a living, in reality you only do one thing—solve problems. For instance, a software engineer solves the problem of efficiently using technology to aid a business, a human resource consultant solves the problem of hiring the right people for the right positions and then ensuring that they are able to work at their highest efficiency, and so on and so forth.

- This is important to remember in running your company. You need to understand what problems an organization has and how your product (you) can solve that problem.

- Research is key for any company to help understand their customers. A company needs to understand their customers better than their customers understand themselves. That way, you not only have an advantage over your competitors, but you can anticipate your customers' problems so that you have no competition.

What does it take to run a company? Are you thinking, "This is for other people, not me. I need security. All I want is a job." Well, guess what? There are no longer 'secure' jobs that last for life. Nobody owes you a living anymore. That is why all employment, in a sense, is evolving to 'self-employment.' We all work for ourselves, even if we are working for a large organization. Here are some things to think about when running a company:

- How many organizations do you know that have only one client? What company is not always trying to secure new customers, even from their competitors? The answer of course is that a company that has only one client would be bankrupt very soon. It is the old adage that if their customer catches a cold, they would catch pneumonia. Likewise, you also need to develop other clients. It may be that that simply means continually networking to expand your contacts. It could mean that you work within the organization to develop champions within different departments who you can work with in different capacities. The idea is that you make the most sales through networking. Network! Network! Network! No matter if you love your job or think it will last forever, continue to expand and build your network. Think about the products that you buy. Aren't you more likely to buy a product that has worked for a friend or colleague than you are to simply buy something 'off-the-shelf'?

- How many companies market their products/services? The answer is that every company has to do some sort of marketing. This is where your resumé comes into play. It is your marketing brochure. Does it properly convey, in a language your potential customers understand, what you can/want to do for them? Is it up-to-date? Does it go beyond simply describing what you did in your job to highlight what you have accomplished? Don't you want to know what a product can do for you by knowing what it has done for others?

- Do companies employ sales agents, and what is their relationship with them? Do they support their sales reps to help them increase their profitability? Do they keep up with the most current trends in the industry and then let their clients know? Who is your sales rep? That is the role of recruiters. They act as your sales representative. Do you have a relationship with a recruiter so that you are aware of changes in the market and what skills you need?

- Do organizations conduct research and continually upgrade their products? The answer, of course, is yes. All organizations, whether they are in the public or private sector, continually strive to improve their products and services. Every organization spends money on research and development, upgrading of staff skills and development of new programs/products/services that meet the ever-changing needs of their customers.

  How are you upgrading your skills? The skills that are in constant demand are really the 'soft skills' (i.e. communication, creative problem solving, leadership, etc.) because they are common to every organization. No matter how advanced your technical skills may be, organizations succeed or fail based on their ability to lead, communicate effectively, adapt to new situations and problems that arise and motivate their staff to succeed.

  According to Paul Romer of Stanford University, the only thing that defies the law of diminishing returns is ideas. There are never too many ideas. It is the same with leaders. All organizations need leaders. So, organizations need these two things to survive—ideas and leaders. Can you create ideas and lead others? Do you need to develop your skills in those areas? You need to constantly upgrade both your hard and soft skills because that is the way to ensure that your product (you) continues to stay in demand—no matter what is happening!

Like many of his co-workers, Robert was laid off during his company's latest round of cutbacks. "We knew it was coming," said Robert. "The company was bleeding and everybody knew that sooner or later most of us were going to get the axe. I felt that because of my difficult relationship with my director, I would probably be getting the axe sooner rather than later."

As is the story over and over again in cases like these, most people react in one of two ways. They either totally check out mentally, putting minimal effort into their jobs (the 'water cooler' effect), or they hunker down at their desks to work even harder proving that they are invaluable to the organization and thus deserve to have their jobs spared.

Robert took a different approach. "I looked at my skills. On one level, I was an over-50 engineer and there are not a lot of job openings for an over-50 engineer. Then I 'oranged' the situation. What did I really want to do and how could I redefine my skills to get me there? I thought about it, but really had no idea what to do. Since I hadn't been laid off yet, I decided to take more courses. While I was there, somebody told me that I would be very good as a coach—that with my experience in working successfully with people, especially technical people, I could become a business coach. It was something that I never really thought about until that moment. The idea struck me so clearly that when I finally did get my pink slip, instead of being down I was hopeful. I used my severance to get myself established and have never looked back since."

The Difference between Flexibility and Creativity

Robert's course of action is a perfect example of *flexibility*. He was open to new possibilities and options, even those he did not think of personally. In this book we have combined the tools from *Flexible Thinker*® with traditional job finding tools because we believe that the most essential career management skill is *flexibility*. If you are flexible, you are able to seize opportunities in the moment as they happen.

You must be creative to be flexible.
You do not have to be flexible to be creative.

The quintessential difference between flexibility and creativity is that with creativity it is up to you to create the ideas. With flexibility, you can build on the ideas of others. It is about creating options, often under pressure, just as Robert did.

There is no doubt that creativity is an important component of flexibility. But there are many very creative people who are not flexible. Like the proverbial bull in a china shop, they just keep going in the same direction no matter how much the circumstances around them have changed. Yes their ideas are brilliant, but they communicate them so poorly or in such a negative way that they simply upset people and their ideas are undermined by others. We all know the clichéd image of temperamental artists who sit around insulting people and moaning about how misunderstood they are by others. Ideas, like careers, need to be constantly adapted to new realities.

Every idea is an option and the more ideas you have, the more the likelihood of success. You are reading this book because you want to become more flexible in your career. If the ideas in this book work to make your career a success, does anybody really care if they were not your 'original' ideas? Sometimes the most flexible people are the ones who go into a situation with no ideas, which makes them open to the options that present themselves. As we said earlier, creativity is an important component to flexibility but it is not the only component. Communication, attitude, knowledge and critical thinking are also essential to flexibility.

As we will discuss later, networks and support groups are also important for career success. This is not just because everybody knows somebody, it is also because these people want to help you succeed and can provide you with the ideas that you can use to find success.

Chapter Three:

What's Stopping You?!?

The measurement of success
is not how much you have won or lost—
it is how much you have learned.

George is a no-nonsense type in his mid-40s. "My advice to my kids," he says in a half-sarcastic manner, "is to all get their degrees in drama."

Drama?!? Isn't that a waste of time, the short road to failure?

"Absolutely not," says George. "Think about it, all the crap they fill these kids getting their MBAs with is obsolete the minute they teach it. Even worse, it was never really true to begin with. At least in drama school they teach you how to present yourself, improvise with what you have and, more importantly, how to market yourself. I mean, nobody ever becomes an actor with the thought that they are going to hold on to the same part for 30 years and get a gold watch and a pension out of it. They become, by the very nature of the profession, entrepreneurs in a very competitive field. Instead of being afraid of the risk, they embrace it because they have a passion. They look to find things that can work instead of cannot. All business schools teach you are why your idea will fail. Then, to make matters worse, they take some half-cocked idea from some academic who has never held a real job in their life and apply it to the real world where people get hurt. Remember the dot-com mess? PhD to me means Piled High and Deep—people who cannot get jobs anywhere else and tell everybody else how to run their businesses and careers. What the universities don't tell people is that their future is dependent on one thing and one thing only—how they solve problems. That is the only reason I hire people, to solve the problems I have, whether those problems are because of people, processes or technology. That's why people hire me. They don't care what I might have done yesterday, they want to know what I can do for them now."

Although George's assessment is harsh, one point that he makes needs to be explored. One of the most sacred pieces of advice that has been handed down from generation to generation is that if you have a business degree or an advanced degree from a university that you will always be employed. The hard skills that a university bestows upon its graduates are the surest way to stay employed throughout your lifetime. While an education is extremely important in developing a strong skill set and the idea of lifetime learning, which we will explain later, is critical to career success, simply getting a degree is no guarantee anymore that you will be able to land the job you want.

George is also right in his assessment that the only way a business will succeed is if it can overcome obstacles. Although it may sound like a very simplistic statement, problem solving is the essence of all business. You are there to solve problems. Problems are made up of a series of obstacles. People give you money to solve their problems. If you create more problems than you solve, then people will not give you their money. All businesses operate on that principle.

It is the same with your business. You only exist to overcome the obstacles that create problems. If there were no problems or obstacles, there would be no jobs. For instance, if you had a job for life and there was no possibility of you ever losing your job, you would not be reading this book. There would be no need to be flexible.

We all have to face obstacles—every person and every organization. These obstacles can either hinder or stimulate our ability to be both creative and flexible. That is why some companies or people do well during downturns, while others go bankrupt during booms. The most in-demand skill in the job market is and always will be the ability to overcome obstacles and solve problems. Your ability to solve problems and document those successes (we will discuss the importance of keeping an accomplishment journal later in the book) has a direct impact on your marketability in the workplace and your ability to manage your career.

Internal Obstacles versus External Obstacles

Flexibility does not exist without obstacles. Success does not exist without obstacles. In fact, the bigger the obstacles are, the greater the success. It is our obstacles that make us flexible.

How can obstacles stimulate our ability to be both creative and flexible?

There are two types of obstacles—external and internal.

External obstacles stimulate our ability to be flexible and help our career management. External obstacles include such things as **time, money, manpower, technology, negative criticism from others** and **competition.** Others direct these obstacles toward us.

Internal obstacles are the obstacles that stop us from being flexible and hinder our career management. These are the obstacles that we create. They include **fear, false ego, complacency no/negativity, and preconceived ideas.** We have total control over them, but often allow them to control us. They have a direct bearing on our decisions, our flexibility, and, ultimately, our success.

Team Obstacles

How many times have you heard about somebody who seemed perfect for a job being turned down because they did not have the 'right degree/experience/qualifications, etc.'? Obstacles like these that you may face in the marketplace can be considered 'team' obstacles. The team in this case is you and a potential employer. A team acts in the same way as an individual, with each person making up a part of the whole. What this means is that a negative person within a team can act in the same way that an internal 'no' acts within an individual—it can stop the process and disrupt the team. So, how do you take a team internal obstacle, which can stop you, and turn it into a team external obstacle, which will trigger your flexibility?

Take a moment and think about a time when you were successful. What were the obstacles that you faced? Were other people who were negative, had preconceived notions, etc. some of the obstacles? Odds are that they made up a huge chunk of your challenge. How did you handle these obstacles? Did you believe what these people said, or did you ignore it or even go around them? By using the tactic of ignoring or going around a person within the team who presents an internal obstacle, you really take that person out of the team. That person then goes from being an internal team obstacle to an external team obstacle. As President of *Me Inc.*, you can listen to the valid criticism of others and use it to improve your product. You cannot, however, get caught up in the obstacles of others. In other words, you cannot make another person's obstacles your own obstacles because by making them your own they become internal obstacles that will stop you.

How These Obstacles Affect Your Career

Although external and internal obstacles were discussed in quite a bit of detail in *The Flexible Thinker®: A Guide to Creative Wealth*, we need to examine how these obstacles can derail your career management. The internal obstacles are the fear of trying something new, the ability to trust enough to say 'yes' to somebody else's ideas, trying to control what others do, etc. These are the obstacles that stop us from being flexible and limit our career choices more than the external obstacles of a tight job market, oversupply of labor, etc. Since the external obstacles (i.e. market conditions, competition, etc.) are so obvious, let's examine in greater detail the internal obstacles and how they can affect the ability to manage your career and find the job you want.

Fear

I never really liked my job, but I was too afraid to move.
I don't know what to do now. I don't know what the future holds.
I've got bills to pay and I cannot be out of work.

Sandy knew the axe was coming. "Every day was like holding your breath," she sighed. "The fear was stifling."

Sandy was a single mom and did not know what to do. "I felt like my head was in a fog. Everyone around me was being laid off, but I did not know what to do. I couldn't be out of a job," she exclaimed.

Did she put her resumé together? Did she contact agencies or colleagues while she had a job? "No, I did not. It just all seemed so overwhelming that I just started going into a deep depression."

Fear is a primal instinct that is common to all beings. It is not logical. Think of this—legend has it that the number one fear for people is public speaking with death the second greatest fear. If this were true, then more people would rather be the corpse than give the eulogy! There is an infinite variety of fears. Some are well-founded and protect us. Others, however, are unfounded and hinder us. It is the old *flight* or *fight* rule. Fear can trigger our creativity when we take the *fight* route. In that sense, it can actually help our careers.

Fear can **help** careers?!? It can if we do something about it. For instance, if you are afraid of losing your 'edge' and then take courses to upgrade your skills so that you remain competitive in the workplace, then fear has actually helped to keep you sharp. The type of fear that hinders creativity is when we are so afraid that we shut down and do nothing—like the deer caught in the car's headlights. We are so afraid of losing our job/moving to something better that we keep doing the same thing without looking for other options.

The 'water cooler syndrome' and 'ghosting' come from fear. You complain about a situation as a substitute for doing something about it. You become so overwhelmed with the fear that you check out mentally in order to deal with it. You then internalize the fear and it becomes depression. You are now on the downward spiral. The fear becomes overwhelming and your desperation is palatable.

How Fear Stops Career Management

- Paralyzes the body and mind and stops us from being able to move forward and manage our careers.
- Creates negative images in our minds that set us up for failure and hinder our search for new employment opportunities.
- Refocuses our energy on alleviating or escaping the fear (the flight syndrome) instead of solving the problem or overcoming the obstacles that are present.

Fear lurks in many places. Sometimes it is instinctual and is used to protect us from places or situations that put our safety in jeopardy. More often, however, it manifests itself as an image of the worst possible scenario. We imagine that the worst that can happen already has and we shut down in order to deal with it. It comes from the unknown and a lack of trust—in our selves, our skills, our environment and our support systems.

How can we deal with *fear*? Here is an exercise from the *The Flexible Thinker®* that is worth trying.

THE WORRY BUSTER

Purpose of exercise:

- Define exactly what you are scared of
- Create peace of mind.

How the exercise works:

Take some time to relax and focus in on what frightens you. It might be losing your job, making a career shift or taking on a new opportunity.

1   Clearly define your worry or concern. (Be careful to include only *real* facts, not *apparent* facts.)

2   Write down (this is very important) what you think is the worst possible outcome.

3   Write down what **specific** steps you will take immediately to begin to improve upon the worst possible outcome.

Does your fear now seem more manageable? Remember that the antidote to worry is creative action. If you are doing something about the fear, it is less likely to be overwhelming.

False Ego

> *I am indispensable to my company.*
> *So–and–so is a 'blankety–blank.'*
> *I'm the only one who knows how to do anything around here.*

Michelle has a habit of irritating people. She is constantly critical about everything. "Oh, that community is such a hick town," she tells her lunch mate in what she thinks is a funny way. Instead of laughing, the lunch mate (whom she knows lives in that town) is simply put off.

The lunch mate then attempts to tell Michelle about his vision for a new company, but Michelle simply tells him over and over again how she won't get involved until she sees the full business plan. She is told that what is wanted at the new company is an environment of mutual support, where each person sets up the other for success. "Well," she comments, "it is easier to do that with bigger companies because when you have a lot of fish in a small pond they tend to nip each other's tails."

Michelle then proceeds to put down a large number of people and finishes by patting herself on the back for "not being one of those whiny people when I don't get what I want". By the end of the meal, Michelle's lunch mate is so turned off that he almost runs out of the restaurant.

Not only did Michelle limit her network by upsetting her lunch mate, she also ultimately lost out on a chance to work for the new company that was described to her that day. It turned out to be successful and would have provided Michelle with an amazing opportunity to fulfill her career goals.

True and False Egos

There are two kinds of egos—true and false. True ego is a very positive attribute. It is a quiet self-confidence that comes from knowing you can do the job and are good at what you do. True ego is marked by humility and allows you to continue to learn and grow because you are not afraid of others. People who possess true ego are supportive because they do not feel threatened. They are also always looking to better themselves because they know that they can always be sharper. They are generous in their knowledge because they are confident in it and know they can learn by sharing. True ego helps people manage their careers successfully because they do not care about limitations placed on them by others.

False ego is characterized by putting others down, either through gossip or intimidation. People with a false ego jealously guard their own power or position because they believe they do not deserve it. They are also envious of others and cannot listen for fear of others finding out their limitations. People with a false ego have limited career opportunities because they obstruct the success of others on the team and ultimately themselves.

False ego limits our choices when we believe there is nothing more to learn, when we are afraid of trying new things because we might look silly, or when we look down on others. We limit our choices.

The 'Dog Urinating around the Tree' Syndrome

The essence of successful career management is building bridges with other people. We will be discussing networking extensively in a later chapter, but essentially, a successful networker is a person who helps others succeed. Like a dog marking its territory, people with false egos tend to mark their territory very carefully and do not allow others to cross over. In the stream of ideas, they are like a dam. Ideas build up behind them. Eventually a few ideas seem to trickle around them and then a few more. Finally they go from being a dam in the stream to an island in the stream. Yes, they have their own territory, but nobody cares anymore because they have found a way around them.

It is normal to get jealous of other people's success. The problem is that when we do that we limit our own career achievements because that person might be able to help us. There is enough success to go around for everybody.

The reason false ego often manifests itself in blocking careers is the need for control. The job market changes and skills that were needed one day may be in great surplus tomorrow.

The Four Signs of a False Ego and How It Stifles Career Management

Judgmental

There is a saying that you are what you do. When you judge others, you are really judging yourself. Judgmental people often indulge in gossip because it allows them to protect their own ego at the expense of someone else. It is almost like they are saying, "See, I'm not so bad because I am better than that person." When you throw dirt, however, some of it always sticks. Career opportunities are oftentimes right in front of you, but if you are always critical you may not see them for what they are.

Overly concerned about the opinion of others

Successful continuous career management comes from having choices. The more options you have, the more likely you will be to find career success. Don't be fooled into limiting your choices by thinking, "I'm too good for that," or "I will never work for my competitor." You are simply confusing bravado and arrogance with self-confidence. Your career may be constricted because you fear looking 'foolish' or even failing and being exposed to ridicule.

Jealousy

When we discuss the CAR technique, we will explore how an important element of career success is the creation of achievements. False ego can hinder your own success in the workforce because jealous people will undermine their co-workers to ensure that others do not achieve more than them, even if it means limiting their own success.

Arrogance

Arrogance is a wonderful defense mechanism. It is defined in the dictionary as being overbearing. It also pushes people and ideas away. An arrogant person wants everyone to believe that he or she knows everything and thus has nothing to learn from others. Successful career management is often dependent on people liking you. There are often several people who have similar hard or technical skills, yet it is the person who can work with others that will move forward.

Complacency

I don't talk to my customers and they don't talk to me.
Eaton's will always be there.

FREDERICK EATON, 1994

(Eaton's, Canada's largest retail outlet, went bankrupt in 2001.)

"I can't believe they outsourced my job," yelled Ken. "They cannot do it half as well as I can."

The problem was that Ken really believed this statement. In the past 30 years, he had not upgraded his education. He did not go out of his way to learn about the latest trends in his industry and he never really risked anything either. He simply kept his head down, his profile low and waited for retirement. Yet, with the world changing so rapidly, he did not see that jobs know no borders and skills have to be continually upgraded.

Why is it that often times new immigrants come to this country without a dime in their pockets and become millionaires while people who were born and educated here end up broke? The simple reason is that people who come here with nothing know that they cannot wait for somebody to give them their opportunity. They have to create it themselves. This is the essence of career management. You can no longer wait for somebody else, whether it is the organization you work for, or the government, to keep your job safe for a lifetime. Here are some interesting facts:

- Over half of the Fortune 500 companies from 1975 no longer exist today. Companies on this list included Eastern Airlines, Pan Am, and Woolworth, etc. Companies not on the list include WalMart, Microsoft and Intel.
- Nobody owes you a job anymore. The idea of lifetime employment has gone the way of the Dodo bird. In fact, companies cannot even guarantee their own existence. According to Arie DeGeus of Harvard University, the average life of a corporation is now half the working life of an individual.

One of the ideas of this program is to get you to think about your career creatively even while under pressure. The very nature of this program suggests urgency. If you are comfortable enough to wait for things to happen to you, this process will not work effectively. It is the difference between managing and controlling your own career, and hoping for charity by waiting for others to do it for you.

How Complacency Stops Career Management

- There is no urgency or need to control your career so you are willing to turn over your career to the whims of others.
- Career growth means taking chances, which is outside the comfort zone. Complacency is the comfort zone.

No/Negativity

I don't do that.
Been there, done that!
No, that will never work.

There is a great scene in the movie *Apollo 13* where the engineers are trying to figure out a way to save the lives of the astronauts. They can tell you why every idea presented will not work. Finally, in exasperation, the character played by Tom Hanks tells them, "I don't want to know what won't work. Tell me something that will!"

"No, that is a bad idea."

"No, that will never work."

We have all heard those sayings. We have probably even said them to ourselves. Like the astronauts whose lives are in peril, we have to find what will work. As we said earlier, career success means having options. Then why limit your options by saying no to all of your possible choices? 'No' as an obstacle means more than just choosing or rejecting an idea, it means that there is a lack of trust. That lack of trust is either between you and others or a personal lack of trust in yourself.

Ways That 'No' Kills Career Management

- Places limitations on the choices presented and the ideas that are created.
- Starts to create a negative environment that stops you from finding the right career opportunity.

Preconceived Ideas

That isn't what I do.
My employer will always take care of me.
If I work harder, I will be able to keep my job forever.
Something must be wrong with me because I lost my job.

Jack was just downsized from his position with an aerospace company.

"From our very first meeting it was clear that Jack was looking for a fight," shares his career coach Ellen exhaustedly. "His style was to be confrontational and at one point he even slammed down his hand on my desk and demanded I answer his question. I did not want him as a client but no one else was available and the account was very valuable to our company."

Ellen *had* to be Jack's career coach and work with him for the next three-month period. She was entrusted with helping him prepare to find a new position. Jack had never worked with a career coach and had already decided from the start that the process was a waste of time. He thought that he was already well versed in looking for work and that there was nothing new for him to learn. Ellen explains that Jack was his own worst enemy. His limited experience and preconceived ideas were a huge handicap in moving forward.

"Jack had only been with the aerospace company for one year. Prior to that he was in the hotel business," comments Ellen. "However, he took time off to complete his MBA and was lucky enough to land a job with a large organization. Unfortunately, he felt that his MBA gave him superior knowledge and that because he had an MBA he would easily land a position over everyone else, even though he had little experience working in corporate environments."

Ellen sighs deeply. "Somewhere along the line Jack was told that an MBA would provide him with lifetime employment and that he would make $100,000 minimum per year," Ellen explains. "Halfway through the three-month program I could see that the arrogant attitude was covering up Jack's insecurities. Realizing that, however, did not lessen the knots in my stomach every time we had a meeting." Jack challenged his consultant on every point and held fast to the ideas he believed were right. He could not be convinced even with hard, cold facts.

Ellen shrugs her shoulders. "I tried everything to convince him that networking was the key to staying employed and his reply was always the same. He would explain that his dad taught him not to ask for favors from anyone and to stand on his own two feet. He would also explain that networking was not part of his culture. His attitude was getting in the way of learning a valuable business skill. After three months of banging my head against a brick wall I admitted defeat. Unfortunately, the long-term result for Jack was that he ended up floating around with no job opportunity trying to make it as a consultant," says Ellen. "The problem with that was he refused to network and every successful consultant knows that the key to success is networking."

Jack had two preconceived ideas that he wanted to hold on to—that an MBA would bring him automatic career success and that networking was asking for favors. Both beliefs were huge career blocks for Jack.

We all hold preconceived ideas—about other people, situations, places and even ourselves. These preconceived ideas help us to quickly make decisions and come to conclusions with very little work. Often times, these beliefs are emotional-based on experience or information that we have received earlier. They are formed in our own libraries. In some cases, these ideas serve us well. For instance, if we have been burned by fire, we have a preconceived idea that we should not simply stick our hands in the fire because they will be burned. The problem comes when we are faced with new facts that run counter to our preconceived ideas. Even though the facts may be irrefutable, we hold onto our preconceived ideas and ignore the facts presented. It is these preconceived ideas that can kill our careers.

There is a great story about some teenaged kids who were throwing matches into a newspaper box. Eventually the newspapers caught fire and the fire department was called. The firefighters got to the box, took out their crowbars, axes, etc. and tried to open the box. A little kid came by on his bicycle, looked at the firefighters trying to pry open the newspaper box and asked them why they didn't simply put in a couple of quarters and open the box. The firefighters looked at each other, shook their heads, found a couple of quarters, put them in the box, opened it and put out the fire.

Sometimes the answer to our career challenges is right in front of us. It may be in the form of advice from a friend, or a piece of news that we hear. Yet, if we hold on to our preconceived ideas, we will never be able to use it.

Did you have trouble redefining the orange and giving it a new use because an orange is an orange and you eat it? Did your preconceived ideas limit you so that even when you renamed the orange, you simply called it the name of another fruit? It is the same with careers. You have to 'go outside the box' by redefining yourself and your skills in order to manage your career.

Ways That Preconceived Ideas Kill Career Management

- Vital information is excluded. The excluder discards anything that does not fit into his or her own narrow definition of the world. Such vital information includes ideas, information, and of course the person or idea that is the target of the prejudice.
- Lack of flexibility. There is strong opposition to change and it is ignored until it is too late. The essence of career management today is having the flexibility to adapt your 'product' to the market to continuously create opportunities for yourself.
- Ability to network is limited because your preconceived ideas leave no room for the opinion or ideas of anybody else.

Exercise

Identify the Obstacles to Managing Your Career

Let's go back to your career.

Take some sticky sheets and write one obstacle per sticky until you list every obstacle that you face in managing your career.

Now, place six pieces of paper on the table in front of you. Write down external obstacles, no, false ego, complacency, preconceived ideas and fear. Place each sticky under a category where you think the obstacle fits. If you think of additional obstacles, you can also add these later and place them in the appropriate category. The first part of being able to tackle a problem is to identify and write down all of the obstacles that make up the challenge. By doing so, you being the process of dealing with the obstacles that are blocking you.

As you go through this book and you get a tool or an idea to meet a challenge, check it off with a marker, but don't cross it out. You can put more than one check mark next to an obstacle. This means is that you have found more than one way to overcome that obstacle.

There is a fine line between an internal obstacle and an external obstacle. If you are confused about what category to put your obstacle in, write it down again on a separate sticky and place it in another category. By writing it in different places, you are breaking down the obstacle into smaller parts and making it easier to overcome.

Do you encounter obstacles in managing your career? The answer, of course, is yes. Everybody does. We face both internal and external obstacles and, at times, they can seem very daunting. Then how do you deal with them? What happens when you apply the 'orange' tool to them? Can you redefine yourself and your skill set to overcome the preconceived ideas of others? For instance, instead of being 'too old' you can define yourself as experienced and efficient which ultimately costs less. (After all, if you have to train somebody to do a job it costs the organization money and can lead to costly mistakes.)

Businesses 'orange' themselves all the time. They need to constantly redefine themselves in order to survive in the marketplace. Take General Electric ('GE') as an example. How much has GE's image changed over the years? They have redefined themselves as a manufacturing and electrical company that does everything from making jet engines to medical imaging to financing. With this different mindset, GE defines itself as a leader in the industry, rather than just a manufacturing company.

Look at the obstacles you have listed and apply the 'orange' tool. Which ones can that tool help you to overcome? Think very specifically about how to apply it. Here is an example:

Obstacle	Idea/Tool to Overcome
Age—Employers think I am too old for the job.	**Orange**—I accept that there will be employers who will not hire me because of my age. I am not old, I am experienced and can come in to do the job much less expensively because I know how to do it. I have redefined myself as quality improvement. I under stand how to do it faster and less expensively because I have done it so often. I can offer expertise as a consultant or on a contract basis. I have redefined myself as flexi ble. I adapt my knowledge to new changes to maximize the organization's investment in me.

This tool will not work for every obstacle. That is okay. Use it for a few. Remember though to think *specifically* about how you can use it to overcome that obstacle. Write down your ideas. Later, as we move to our action plan, you will be incorporating many of the ideas you have to overcome obstacles into a strategy to continuously manage your career and overcome your obstacles.

Chapter Four:

Marketing Material for *Me Inc.* — The Resumé

When I stand before God at the end of my life, I would hope that I would not have a single bit of talent left and could say, "I used everything you gave me."
—ERMA BOMBECK

Sandra smiles as she thinks about some of the jobs she has done. "In 1994 companies across the globe were striving to keep up with the latest in technology and process. The Fortune 500 Company I worked for was following suit and made the business decision to implement ISO 9003 to stay one step ahead of its competitors. I was chosen to be part of a branch team that would implement and prepare for the ISO audit that would take place in six months time. We worked night and day cleaning out files and following the directions of the head office implementation team point by point to make sure that all of our T's were crossed and our I's were dotted. There was no stone left unturned. Each file in our data bank was reviewed with a fine-tooth comb. The process was reviewed again and again to make sure we were adhering to every rule and regulation that was laid out by the company.

"At the midway point, the branch was subjected to a mock audit by head office to ensure that we were on track. The team went back to the drawing board to correct any inefficiencies in the process. Failure on the day of the audit was not an option. Finally audit day arrived and all eyes were on our branch with my team accountable for the success or failure of the initiative. We all tried to stay calm as the auditors came to sit with each one of us and review our day-to-day work processes. All the hours of labor and stress had cumulated into that one day.

"At the end of the day we received word that our hard work and efforts had paid off and that we had successfully implemented ISO 9003. The branch manager popped the champagne bottles and we toasted to our success with a sigh of relief.

"My co-worker Stacy then turned to me and said that the ISO implementation would certainly be a great addition to our resumés. After all, experience working in an environment that is ISO registered is part of a skill set that is in high demand in the marketplace. In addition, if you have taken part in an implementation process, your knowledge is considered even more valuable.

"When Stacy mentioned that this would be a great addition to our skill set and would give us a marketing edge if we were to look for a job, I stopped and wondered if this was a skill that I wanted to sell to a future employer. Yes, I had slept and eaten ISO, but I hated every minute of it. I am not a real 'process' type of person!"

Sandra makes a very good point. If she was to place this recent accomplishment front and center on her resumé with the intention of attracting potential employers, she would be selling the wrong bill of goods and the employer would be hiring the wrong person. The issue was that she did not enjoy either the audit or the implementation process. Sandra is not an individual who likes details and the whole experience did not work to her strengths or to what she enjoys doing. It was not just the ISO. It could have been any process that was being implemented. Sandra just felt that this was not where she wanted her career to lead. She realized that she could never use her ISO experience as a way to attract an employer because if she did she would most certainly be setting herself up for failure in her next position. What she could do was acknowledge the experience, but not let it overshadow the accomplishments and skills that she excelled at and enjoyed.

The Role of a Resumé as a Marketing Tool for Me Inc.

A resumé must be written with laser focus. The idea of the resumé is to market yourself with the intention of moving your career forward in the direction you want it to go in. If you have sales experience but you do not want to do sales, why would you advertise this front and center on your resumé/marketing piece? Instead, you should highlight the accomplishments that represent the skills you want to use to move forward and achieve your goals. This takes time and can be thought-provoking. The end result, however, is a resumé that has been written with intention. The resumé can then be used as a marketing tool that targets the position you are seeking as well as the skills, knowledge and experience you want to use. It is more than just about what you can do, it is about what you **want** to do. What you want to do and what you have done can be two different things.

Many people believe that a resumé is something you pull out

and dust off whenever you are looking for a new position. All you have to do is add the job description of your last position! This is no longer the case. You must look at your resumé as a marketing piece that advertises what it is you can accomplish by stating what results you have yielded from past experiences.

The resumé for *Me Inc.* is an essential component of a marketing campaign. The purpose of a marketing campaign is to create the need for a product or service and to engage and capture your customer's attention. A well-produced resumé, like a well-produced advertisement, can be used to motivate the individual who is reading it.

Investigate the Current Styles and Trends for Resumé Writing

Robert phoned the recruiter as per the advice of his former employer. He had just been downsized from his five-year senior project manager position with an aerospace company. The conversation went well and the recruiter seemed to think that she might have a contract position that would be suitable. The recruiter requested that Robert e-mail his resumé as soon as possible and, after she reviewed the resumé, would set up an appointment for some time later that week.

The next morning the recruiter called and in no uncertain terms told Robert that his resumé embodied everything you should not do on a resumé. She told him that there is no way she could present the resumé to her client. At first Robert felt defensive and stated that he had used a style that had brought him success in the past. The recruiter's response was, "Five years ago—is that what you mean?" The recruiter went on to explain to Robert that if he had not been introduced to her and instead had sent in his resumé blind, she would not even have considered him for this position, or any other position she was presently working on.

Robert had clearly not taken the time to investigate current styles of resumé writing. Instead, he assumed that the resumé that had worked for him five years ago would bring him the same success. This book is not about resumé writing. There are hundreds of books on this subject in bookstores and libraries around the world. Our focus is to increase your understanding of the importance of the resumé as a marketing tool. The following information will help you to stay current with styles so that your resumé captures and engages the reader's attention.

The Power of a Resumé

Walk around with a resumé in your back pocket at all times.

Not having a resumé is the number one reason people feel they are stuck in a job/position. The number one reason for not having a resumé is, "I don't have the time to write one." The irony is that today you can't afford not to have one.

How would it feel to have a resumé that is up-to-date and successfully speaks to your accomplishments? Wouldn't it allow you to feel less fear and more in control of your career?

Investigate the current styles and trends for resumé writing

The look of a resumé can date you immediately. Nothing says 'behind the times' more than an old-fashioned resumé. It can also make it seem like you have not even bothered trying to keep up with market trends. A resumé is a work in progress, not something you dust off every few years in order to add your latest experiences.

The best way to keep track of current resumé trends is to head to the bookstore or library, or to search the Internet. There are hundreds of books on this subject. I suggest you find a book that relates to your local market. Recruiters are also a great source of information and can give you some pointers.

The following is a list of some of the latest market information on resumé writing.

1 Two pages are all that is required.
2 Check for spelling and grammar. Have two friends check your resumé as well!

3   Most human resources professionals and recruiters are not interested in information that is more than 10 years old. Do not include outdated information.

4   Education should be at the end of the resumé not the beginning.

5   Resumés should clearly state your achievements and accomplishments in combination with a brief outline of responsibilities.

6   Hard skills such as up-to-date technical and computer competencies should be showcased on your resumé.

7   Investigate and understand the current trends of how resumé retrieval systems and technology accept your resumé.

Apply for a position at least once a year.

No matter how secure you think your present position is, would it not be comforting to know just how marketable you really are? It is not disloyal to your present employer to keep your eye on the market—it is savvy career management. After all, the best time to find out if you are actually marketable is when you are employed. What would happen if you sent your resumé out to recruiters and posted your resumé on the Internet and you got no response?

If you receive no response, ask the following questions and take the necessary action:

- Are my skills, education, knowledge and experience in line with what employers are looking for?
- Is my resumé capturing and marketing my skills and accomplishments in a current and proper format?
- Do I have the current hard skills, systems, processes, computer and technical skills that are important to my target market?

A resumé is the tool that gives you the power to move forward in the 21st century workforce.

The Value of Listing Your Accomplishments and Keeping an Accomplishment Journal

After the loss of her position as a marketing manager for a large international appliance company, Irene was both devastated and excited about looking for a new position. She met with her career consultant and it was determined that the first course of action was to start writing her resumé. It had been three years since she had written her last one and she needed a resumé that was more in line with current trends in the marketplace.

Irene left her career consultant's office excited about writing a marketing brochure that focused on her accomplishments and did not just list her job responsibilities. When the consultant did not hear back from Irene, she called her client to see how she was doing with the resumé writing process. Irene was frustrated and embarrassed that she had not been able to finish writing about what she had achieved in her last two positions. "I felt awful. I could not remember what I had done and what the results were. I went to work and I did my job and while I was doing it, I was not thinking about how this information would be crucial to my next career move. My focus was not on me, but on the company I was working for at the present time."

Irene is not alone in her frustration. In our coaching practice and during workshops we meet people everyday that have the same reaction as Irene when it comes to sitting down and writing a resumé. Resumés have slowly changed over the years from a piece of paper that lists duties and responsibilities to a document that requires us to list what we actually did within the boundaries of the duties and responsibilities. This allows other people to understand the results of our work/projects.

Everyone gets a job description that includes duties, responsibilities and expectations. What you accomplish within those guidelines is what will set you apart from other people in the workplace. The number one style of interviewing is the behavioural interview. In order to be successful you must be able to articulate and give examples of your accomplishments, how you solved problems, met deadlines and improved systems and processes, etc.

The most efficient way to track this information is through an *Accomplishment Journal*. By using this tool on a regular basis (every quarter or after the completion of a project), you will save yourself a considerable amount of time and effort when it comes time to sit down and write or update your resumé. The *Accomplishment Journal* can also be used for the purpose of an internal corporate yearly review. How would it feel to sit in front of your manager and give a list of your contributions and accomplishments combined with the results for the year? Wouldn't it relieve stress and allow you to take control of the review? By listing and documenting your accomplishments, you are helping to empower yourself and take control of your career.

The following are examples of specifics you should be tracking:

1   Developed continuous process improvements within billing production, resulting in invoices being delivered to customers in an accurate and timely fashion.

2   Managed the implementation of projects including system enhancement and process re-engineering, which improved company results and objectives for the year 2001.

3   Co-ordinated the logistics of building new telecommunications systems for six new office sites across Canada within four months—'on cost' and 'on time.'

4   Reorganized the filing system to ensure easy access to corporate documents.

5   Increased sales by 20 percent by implementing a national sales and marketing campaign.

6   Created a marketing plan that increased sales by 20 percent.

7   Devised action plans to resolve a myriad of tricky situations and bring teams of people together to carry out these plans, ensuring continued customer satisfaction.

8   Reduced receivables from 48 to 32 days by creating and implementing a new follow-up process.

9   Successfully co-coordinated and managed the administration and report production of 28 sales representatives.

The trick is to review your Accomplishment Journal every quarter. If you find, time and time again, that you do not have any accomplishments to speak of, ask yourself some tough questions:

- Is my present position allowing me the opportunity to gain the experience and knowledge I need to keep my career on the move and be prepared for the future?
- Will I be able to answer behavioral type questions during the interview process?
- Is my career standing still—am I just doing my job and filling in time?

If you are not learning new skills, gaining knowledge, keeping up with new technology, processes and systems you may be committing career suicide. Unfortunately, you will have to pay the price when you start to look for your next position. Remember, even Bill Gates has to tell his shareholders what his company has accomplished every quarter.

How to Use the C.A.R. Method to Effectively Communicate Accomplishments

C.A.R. means Challenge Action Result. Some other acronyms that mean something similar include S.T.A.R (Situation, Task, Action, Result) or PAR (Problem, Action, Result). For us, C.A.R. is the vehicle that allows you to track, write and articulate your accomplishments and the results. C.A.R. is used in the Accomplishment Journal to track information regarding your work and its outcome, and can then be used to write that statement on your resumé and to communicate the information during the interview process.

It's Time to Sell Your C.A.R.!!!!

- What was the **CHALLENGE**?
- What was the **ACTION** you took to meet the challenge?
- What was the **RESULT**?

> - **CHALLENGE**
> - **ACTION**
> - **RESULT**

To own a C.A.R. is to understand bottom line accountability and to be able to convey that to others.

Prove Your Value

Hiring managers scan your resumé looking for clues about what type of worker you are. If you show that you consistently produced positive results for previous employers, you will be seen as a desirable candidate. The key is to emphasize your accomplishments and provide proof of your potential value.

Quantify Results

Which statement has more impact?

A Significantly increased revenues and grew client base.

B Increased revenues from $250,000 in 1997 to $1.5 million in 2000 and tripled client base from 2,500 to 7,000.

In both cases, the candidate is trying to convey how s/he increased revenues and expanded the client base, but statement B measures how well s/he achieved this growth. Wherever possible, include measurable results of your work.

Note that not everyone can release company performance figures. If presenting this information is a breach of confidentiality, find another way to present your accomplishments. For example, use percentages rather than actual dollar figures.

Examples of Accomplishment Statements:

➤ Reduced the annual security operating budget by 22 percent by developing and implementing several cost savings projects while increasing the level of security.

➤ Reorganized and consolidated accounting, analysis and forecasting activities, achieving a $50,000 annual cost saving.

➤ Systematized a manual system for order intake, saving eight processing days per month.

➤ Created and conducted a selection interview training program for managers and supervisors, reducing candidate selection ratio from 1:15 to 1:5.

➤ Reduced internal product rejections from 14 percent of sales to 2 percent and customer quality returns from 3 percent to 0.1 percent.

➤ Initiated an Employee Opinion Survey that resulted in the implementation of new policies and procedures and significantly increased morale.

➤ Reduced receivables from 45 days to 30 days.

➤ Increased sales activities with new prospects and static accounts, expanding sales by 35%.

➤ Designed equipment and techniques for a new chemical process that raised product market potential from $1 million to over $12 million per year.

➤ Devised an e-mail registry that saved management 12 percent of their discretionary time.

You are What You Write!

The effectiveness of your resumé and how it markets your strengths is very dependent on the words that you choose. Whenever possible, you should use power action verbs. These verbs strongly convey results. Here is a partial list of power action verbs that you can use in your C.A.R. statements.

Accomplished	Critiqued	Influenced	Recommended
Achieved	Cut	Informed	Reconciled
Acted	Decreased	Initiated	Recorded
Adapted	Delegated	Innovated	Recruited
Addressed	Demonstrated	Inspected	Reduced
Administered	Designed	Installed	Referred
Advanced	Devised	Instigated	Regulated
Advised	Diagnosed	Instituted	Rehabilitated
Allocated	Directed	Instructed	Remodeled
Analyzed	Dispatched	Integrated	Repaired
Appraised	Distinguished	Interpreted	Represented
Approved	Diversified	Interviewed	Researched
Arranged	Drafted	Introduced	Restored
Assembled	Edited	Invented	Restructured
Assigned	Educated	Launched	Retrieved
Attained	Eliminated	Lectured	Revitalized
Audited	Enabled	Led	Saved
Authored	Encouraged	Maintained	Scheduled
Automated	Engineered	Managed	Schooled
Balanced	Enlisted	Marketed	Screened
Budgeted	Established	Mediated	Set
Built	Evaluated	Moderated	Shaped
Calculated	Examined	Monitored	Solidified
Catalogued	Executed	Motivated	Specified
Chaired	Expanded	Negotiated	Stimulated
Clarified	Expedited	Operated	Streamlined
Classified	Explained	Organized	Strengthened
Coached	Extracted	Originated	Summarized
Collected	Fabricated	Overhauled	Supervised
Compiled	Facilitated	Oversaw	Surveyed
Completed	Familiarized	Performed	Systemized
Composed	Fashioned	Persuaded	Tabulated
Computed	Focused	Prepared	Taught
Conceptualized	Forecast	Presented	Trained
Conducted	Formulated	Prioritized	Translated
Consolidated	Founded	Processed	Traveled
Contained	Generated	Produced	Trimmed
Contracted	Guided	Programmed	Upgraded
Contributed	HeadedUp	Projected	Validated
Controlled	Identified	Promoted	Worked
Coordinated	Illustrated	Provided	Wrote
Corresponded	Improved	Publicized	
Counseled	Increased	Published	
Created	Indoctrinated	Purchased	

Exercise

Write Your Accomplishments

Write up to five accomplishment statements for your last two positions (don't forget to refer to your **Action Verb List** and the example accomplishment statements above).

Now, write your own **C.A.R.** statement.

Challenge

_____

Action

_____

Result

_____

Profile Your C.A.R.

A profile is a statement that captures the sum total of your experience, skills, expertise and knowledge that you wish to market to a potential employer. It is important to use key words that will be picked up by resumé retrieval systems. Many people assume that an objective should be stated at the beginning of a resumé. This, however, can be very limiting. It may rule you out of potential positions because you have made a statement that stops the reader from further investigating your background and abilities. Individuals with five or more years of work experience should have a profile. An objective should only be used when you are searching for a very specific position and even then it can be combined with the profile resumé.

Profiles

Here are some examples of Profile statements:

➤ A corporate administrative assistant/sales support specialist with extensive experience in database management, teamwork, computer and interpersonal skills. Major strengths in leadership, organization, detail, plus verbal and written communication skills. Exercises exceptional judgment and works independently. A well-organized, results-oriented, dependable professional who takes pride in work. Skilled in Word, Excel, PowerPoint, Access and Outlook. Trained in Microsoft Project, Print Shop and Print Master Deluxe.

➤ A senior level, results-oriented sales professional with nearly 20 years experience in the consumer electronics industry including direct P&L responsibility. Extensive experience in all facets of sales management and in developing and implementing highly successful marketing and promotional programs. Strengths include a strong customer focus and a keen ability to foster productive cross-functional and customer relationships. Strong selling, negotiating, communication and interpersonal skills. A results-oriented individual who executes sound strategies for their profitable exploitation and who develops and motivates people to achieve significant goals.

➤ Degreed computer specialist recognized as expert in providing PC support for top selling office products, fax and e-mail software. Background encompasses help desk level III support, evaluation, justification, sales automation, rollout, training, central database administration and continuous support.

➤ Masters in Computer Science.
  - Identifying automation solutions.
  - Designing and developing varied business applications.
  - Assessing Information Technology needs.
  - Project management including defining standards and policies.

- Expertise includes: Windows, DOS, ACT, Microsoft Office, Lotus 1-2-3, Excel, and Word.
- Extensive knowledge of field sales management and information systems.
- Maintained master database of 28,000 customers.

➤ Diversified experience in the development, creation and coordination of event sponsorship and literature; interfacing with outside advertising agencies and vendors. Strong interpersonal skills, communication skills and computer literate.

➤ Accomplished professional in help desk support, call center administration and customer service communications. Proven strengths include exceptional organizational ability and excellent written and verbal communication. Proficient in SAP/R#, AS400 applications and Vantive call center support tools. Dependable, versatile and conscientious. Knowledgeable in Excel, Word, Lotus, Lotus Notes and Windows.

➤ A human resources professional with 15 plus years of diverse experience, noted for sound judgment and superior interpersonal skills. Generalist experience includes Mergers/Acquisitions, Retirement Savings Pension Program (DCPP, DPSP, EPSP and RRSP) and Flex Benefits Program design and implementation, STD/LTD management, EAP, Facilitation, HRIS, Compensation/Salary Administration, Incentive Programs, Policies and Procedures, Recruitment/Selection and Strong Customer Service.

➤ An enthusiastic and energetic professional with over 14 years experience in the career management, staffing and training fields. A highly effective communicator with strong written and public speaking skills. A project manager and team collaborator with the unique ability to be instrumental in all facets of workshop/seminar creation and implementation combined with sales knowledge and expertise to deliver a profitable outcome.

➤ A respected human resources manager with a proactive and highly supportive leadership style. Excels in building and maintaining relationships at all levels of an organization. Provides value-added consulting services through partnering with line management to align people goals with department and corporate goals. Ability and flexibility to adapt to changing environments

➤ A hard-working, conscientious and dependable worker with over ten years of experience in a variety of factory, labor and moving positions. Able to learn new skills quickly.

➤ A highly respected property manager with a proactive and highly supportive leadership style. Over 15 years experience in all facets of managing residential apartment buildings. An effective communicator both, written and verbally, with the unique ability to be instrumental in all areas of property management including on-site management and accounting. Knowledge and expertise to recognize opportunities to add value and problem solving resulting in a profitable outcome.

Exercise

Now write your profile statement.

It can be helpful to write more than one profile if you need to customize your resumé to a specific position.

Flexible Thinker Tool #2

I Want

Now that you have written your C.A.R. statement, take a moment to look beneath what you have written. How were you able to achieve those results? You certainly faced a number of external obstacles. In fact, that is what made up the essence of the 'challenge' part of the C.A.R. statement. The question is, though, what led to the result? Why is it that you were able to overcome the obstacles this time, when other times you were unable to? Read all of your C.A.R. statements and you will discover an underlying truth in each one:

You were able to overcome the obstacles you faced because you were MOTIVATED to overcome them.

This sounds like a simple statement of truth, yet it is profound. When you had a strong I Want, you were able to overcome significant obstacles in order to achieve the 'result' part of your statement.

Here is an exercise to determine how you can consistently achieve the 'results' you want. Ask yourself these three questions:

1 What motivated you in each of your C.A.R. statements? Was it only money, for example, or something else—like the challenge of succeeding?

2 Were there other people that you were dependent on in order to achieve your result?

3 What motivated them to help you?

By answering these three simple questions, you can begin to understand both what motivates you and what motivates others.

Your second tool—*I Want*
I Want means *Motivation*

Brian has a difficult challenge on his hands. He is told to cut over-time on his team by 50 percent. "I am the meat on the sandwich," Brian sighs. "Above me, I have a manager who has no idea what I do, and below me I have unionized staff members who don't care what I have to say. If there is a problem, they threaten me with a grievance. I have one guy, for instance, who is getting paid on aver-age with overtime 22 hours a day, seven days a week, 365 days a year. He's sleeping on the job four hours a day and there is nothing I can do about it. His brother's the shop steward!" He sighs. "What am I supposed to do to motivate *them*?!?"

We talk about how to use the *I Want* tool and Brian becomes agitated. "Yeah, that stuff is great in theory BUT it doesn't work in the real world."

We then ask Brian what motivates him. "I'll tell you what motivates me," Brian says with a smirk. "A big screen TV! That's what motivates me." Well, if that is what motivates you, then the chances are that it might motivate others.

Brian then gets an idea. Perhaps he can *orange* the overtime challenge by making it into a game. "We can set up a pool where, if we decrease overtime by 50 percent, we can have a party for everybody and give away a big screen television."

He then takes the plan to his manager. He estimates that the cost of the party—including the price of a big screen television—would be approximately $7,000. If he cuts overtime by 50 percent, the savings to the company would be $150,000. When he present-ed the math to his manager, the manager immediately gave him permission to go ahead. "After all," Brian says, "he is on profit sharing, so he has an *I Want* too."

We followed up with Brian six months later to find out how his plan worked. "It was amazing," Brian exclaimed. "The entire group really got into it. They kept score and they even developed an inter-nal competition that was fun. It was also interesting how they dealt with the one member whom I told you who was making all of that overtime. Well, the other members of the team started waking him up every few minutes when he went to sleep and then they started leaving him alone in not the safest circumstances. He finally got the message and his overtime decreased dramatically. In fact, overtime didn't just fall by 50 percent, we ended up decreasing it by 70 percent and were able to give away two big screen televisions."

As Brian learned, what motivates people is not simply money. This is an emotional tool, not a logical one. Sometimes what motivates people can be illogical, resulting in secret agendas.

What Do You Want?

> *People would do for a piece of ribbon what they would never in a million years do for money.*
> —Gen. Omar Bradley

In a famous University of Southern California study, two groups of people were given the same menial task. One group was paid $5 an hour and the other group was not paid. In each case, the group that was not paid performed better than the group that was paid $5 an hour.

The U.S.C. experiment found that the six strongest causes of motivation were*:

1 Challenge
2 Love
3 Respect
4 Dependence on others
5 Fear
6 Money.

This is important to think about when you are managing your career. What is it that motivates you to perform and motivates others to help you succeed? Do you motivate others through a shared sense of values and respect or through intimidation and control?

---

* U.S.C. Department of Behavioral Sciences

The experiment was originally conducted to test Maslow's Hierarchy of Needs. Maslow's Hierarchy of Needs basically states that people are more motivated as they reach the top of a pyramid. The motivators are:

1   **Basic needs.** This is the 'money' need. We need money to pay for basic necessities such as clothes, food and shelter. We need to take care of this need before we move to the next need. For example, if a person is starving, his/her immediate interest is to get food, not to achieve something great for mankind.

2   **Safety.** We need to feel safe. If there was a fire, our energies would be devoted to finding a safe place where the fire could not harm us.

3   **Psychological.** We are creatures who need other people in our lives. After all, no person is an island. We need to belong and feel safe, not only in a physical sense, but also in an emotional sense. We are therefore more motivated to help when we feel that we are 'part of the group' or when we feel good about what we are doing.

4   **Respect.** A higher psychological form. When we are respected and valued, we perform in accordance with those expectations. There is an old saying that you will succeed for somebody who believes you can succeed. This is very true in the workplace. When we work with or for somebody who respects us, our productivity rises significantly. Respect is one of those things that the more you give away, the more you have. We respect people who respect us.

5   **Self-Actualization.** This is the challenge—"I had to do it because I knew I could." This is the highest of all motivators. People are most motivated when they internalize a challenge and make it their own. Look at your C.A.R. statements. How many of them were done *in spite* of what people thought? Their opinions didn't matter because you had to prove to yourself that you could do it.

Although there are times in our careers where we are focused on the lower levels of Maslow (i.e. you just need a job to pay the bills and are afraid of making ends meet because you do not have enough money coming in, etc.), it is important to try to look 'beyond the treadmill' at the upper levels of Maslow to help guide your career.

How 'I Want' Affects Your Career and Resumé

What do you want to be when you grow up? That is as good a question to ask now as when you were 10 years old. What is it that you want to do, and does your resumé reflect this? It is like the I.S.O. story we discussed above. Are you using your accomplishments and C.A.R. statement to sell your product/ services to the company that needs them? It is the same as selling laundry detergent. The people who manufacture laundry detergent want to sell their product to people who need to clean their clothes. In other words, they are marketing the product to potential clients who have that need. Are you using your resumé to motivate others to hire your services to meet their needs, or are you simply motivated at the lower levels of Maslow—in other words, you need a job to simply meet your basic needs. What will your motivation be like?

Have you ever worked for or with somebody who is not motivated or motivated negatively? How does that affect the environment? His or her lack of motivation affects everybody around him/her. What happens when you use your resumé to get a job that you do not really want? Odds are that you will not do a very good job, and both parties will become frustrated with each other. It is the same when you buy a product that does not work in the way that it was promised. You quickly form a negative impression of the whole company and do not want buy their products again.

Exercise

Using 'I Want' to Help You

- What are the '*I Wants*' in your career?
- How can you express them in your resumé to motivate others to help/hire you?

Remember that you cannot motivate others unless you are motivated first!

The answers to these questions will help you put together your resumé in a way that markets not simply what you can do, but what you want to do. By combining your C.A.R. statements with your Accomplishment Journal and then having a clear idea of what you want to do, you will be able to take control of your career instead of reacting to external forces that you cannot control.

Some final points to remember about resumés...

➤ It is important to understand the technical aspects of online job applications.

➤ You should use your resumé to test your marketability even when you are happily employed. That way you know your worth and what skills you need to stay on the cutting edge.

➤ Your resumé can create the I Want in others to help you go from where you are to where you want to be!

Your resumé is a key component of the marketing strategy of *Me Inc.* It is a marketing brochure. Make sure it reflects the newest, improved model of your product—you!

Go back and examine the obstacles you listed previously. What new ideas can you apply to help overcome them? Remember to think very specifically about either the idea, or how you can apply your new tools to overcome that obstacle. Look at all of your obstacles, even ones you may have checked off earlier. The more ideas you have to overcome an obstacle, the more likely that that obstacle will never stand in your way again.

Chapter Five:

Marketing Me Inc. Action Plan

Quantum results need quantum ideas.

Combining Different Marketing Avenues for Career Success

Doug is a software developer with ten years experience. He had successfully completed his resumé, prepared his references and begun his job search. After a month of posting his resumé on all of the job boards and contacting three agencies, he had not landed a single interview. In frustration, he approached a career management consultant to discuss how he could expand his job search.

During the first meeting, Doug explained to the consultant that he had always had success with the Internet over the years. Also, he had received countless calls from recruiters approaching him with opportunities while he was working, so he could not believe the lack of response from this search. Doug was beginning to believe his resumé could be at fault. Even worse, he wondered if his lack of success had something do to with him personally.

When he was downsized from his former company, he did not expect that he would have this much trouble finding a position. After all, he had moved several times over the last ten years and had always received an immediate response from the Internet. But this time, Doug had applied for over 50 positions and completed at least 30 online corporate applications and had come to a dead end at every turn. He was now worried what the future would bring if he did not land a position within the next few months. When he was asked if he had been networking, his response was that he had contacted a number of individuals with whom he had worked over the years. He had given them his resumé asking the contacts to let him know if they heard of anything.

Doug had made the typical mistake that many job seekers make during the search process. He had put all his eggs in one basket—in this case, the Internet. The reason he had focused on the Internet so exclusively was because that had been a successful approach for him in the past—in a market where there were more jobs than applicants. However, Doug was now conducting a job search in an employers' market—a market where there are more applicants than jobs. Doug had not taken into account that the market had dramatically changed over the last two years and that he needed to expand his resources.

The Internet is a wonderful tool. However, it is only one of many tools that need to be utilized during a work search campaign. Doug had become an island unto himself, sending a message out into a vast wasteland of cyberspace, hoping that someone would respond. He had virtually given the future of his career over to one small piece of the job search process. When unsuccessful, job searching on the Internet can be frustrating and can cause self-doubt, leaving a person with a sense of isolation that cyberspace can create.

Job Search Statistics

- 5 percent of positions come from the Internet
- 15 percent to 20 percent+ of positions come from recruiters
- 60 percent+ of positions come from networking

Doug is not alone. Unfortunately, 80 percent of the people spend 80 percent of their time in an area that yields only 5 percent of the results. When asked why, most people say that this method has worked for them in the past. Other reasons include, "I hate networking" or, "I have had bad experiences with recruiters." Yet, if we were to ask any manager how he or she would deal with an employee that focuses his or her energies on trying to complete a project using only 5 percent of the resources available and fails, his/her answer would most likely be that that person would not be at his or her job for long.

As is the case for any marketing campaign, you need an action plan that gives your product or service the best chance to be exposed to as many avenues as possible. You cannot possibly hope to sell an important product or service by advertising in just one area. This can limit your market potential. As CEO and President of *Me Inc.*, you must take out your sales and marketing hat and, with laser focus, implement your work search marketing campaign. The quote at the beginning of this chapter, "Quantum results need quantum action" is a rule to live by if you want to have choices. You have to create those choices by venturing down all avenues available.

The 10% Sales Rule

There is a general rule that for every 100 brochures you send out, you will be required to make 100 follow-up calls to create 10 face-to-face appointments that may land one sale.

There are a number of variables attached to this rule—the product, the region, the economy, etc. Sometimes the salesperson will get lucky and make an immediate sale, but many times it will take a lot more than 100 phone calls to create the 10 face-to-face meetings necessary to land the sale. The idea behind this rule is that it is a good measurement of what it will take for you to reach your ultimate goal of landing the right position.

The Four Step Guide to Career Marketability

The following four steps—*Networking*, *Recruiters*, *Target Marketing* and the *Internet*—are individually discussed to give you a complete step-by-step outline that you can use to master each technique. At the end of this chapter, you will be given instructions on how to implement a *career search action* plan that will help you measure and maximize your results.

Step One—*Networking*

Are you familiar with the theory of *Six Degrees of Separation?* The premise behind this theory is that everyone on the planet is indirectly connected to one another by a string of friends and relationships that does not exceed six people. For instance, no matter if the person is an aboriginal in a South American rainforest or the President of the United States, you can connect yourself directly to him or her by a string that is no greater than six degrees (i.e. a friend of a friend of a friend, etc.).

Networking Is Not Instant Gratification

The importance of networking to your career as a whole cannot be stressed enough. Networking is not only useful when you are looking for a job, it is a commitment that continues throughout the lifetime of your career. Networking should be part of career management whether you work for yourself, or want to work for somebody else. As we all know, it isn't what you know, it's who you know! Networking is what gets you noticed when you are working for a corporation. It is the essential element of running your own company—*Me Inc.*! After all, how many businesses do you know that only have one customer? Networking allows you to develop a number of customers/potential customers so that you will always be in demand no matter what the market is like.

Take the case of Joe and Mark. Joe keeps his nose to the grindstone at work. He does not have time to take lunch or get involved with water cooler gossip. He is a hard worker, exceptionally knowledgeable and is recognized as the individual you can always go to if you need information. When people go to Joe and ask him to share information or give direction or help, Joe will always willingly oblige. Project leaders in the company are always happy to have Joe as a member of their team because he is known as a team player that can get the job done.

Mark is also a good worker. He, however, in no way has the knowledge or experience that Joe has, but he is well liked. Mark makes a point of taking the time to cruise the different departments within the organization to say hello and share a moment of conversation. He knows the vice president in marketing, has lunch with the director of finance, and remembers the name of the president's administrative assistant's grandchildren. Once a week he stops by his manager's office and updates the manager on the progress of the projects he is working on. He makes sure to share his successes, all the while soliciting advice and gaining approval for his decisions. He always invites his manager to join him for lunch to discuss upcoming projects.

A new management position has opened up and both Mark and Joe apply for it. Who do you think gets the job? When we ask this question during workshops and seminars, no one ever answers, "Joe." Most people think that Mark will get the promotion because he is 'sucking up' or, in some way, manipulating the situation and the boss. In their opinion, Joe deserves the position because he works harder, but they know from experience that it will be Mark.

Here is a question to think about. Is Mark 'sucking up' to his superiors, or is he strategically placing himself in a position where people are aware of his contributions to the company?

Networking within the Organization

Irene, a recently downsized sales manager from the telecommunications industry, could relate to Joe. She was the hard worker who never tooted her own horn. She simply did the best work she could in a modest way. She had always assumed that the organization would take care of her. Irene is now learning the importance of managing her own career and not handing her future over to others.

"Prior to my departure from the company, I viewed career management skills such as networking almost as a waste of time and just focused on day-to-day operations," Irene says with a long sigh. "My recent experiences have since created an overwhelming change in attitude. I now see that networking and career management are not only a priority, they are also a mandatory part of any career. Networking, especially, is a long- term commitment."

What Is Networking?

Networking is about exchanging information, not about asking for a job.

During a job search most people start with their immediate circle of friends and business connections. The most common approach is to let people know you are looking for a new position and then to send your resumé to them in the hopes that if they know of a possible opportunity they will pass your resumé on to the person that is hiring. The problem with this approach is that you give away your power and control over the process. Most people have great intentions and want to help, but they also have heavy workloads and other activities that take their focus away from your resumé and job search. You need to ask different questions so that you are in complete control of the process.

Asking a question about what positions are available creates yes or no answers. For instance, you can ask your contacts for their opinion on the hiring trends of the company in the future. This creates dialogue and takes the pressure off the person if there is nothing available immediately.

Salespeople who are selling large items or services know that they will not get the sale during the first conversation. First, they have to build the relationship. If you create the relationship first, you are more likely to be remembered if something comes along in the future. Even if you make contacts during a job search that seem to have no value at the immediate point of contact, consider them as opportunities to build relationships and continue to exchange information in the years to come. Remember that the average position lasts 2.5 years.

The following is a list of powerful networking questions you can ask. Instead of a closed question (one with a simple yes or no answer), these are open questions designed to help you develop a dialogue with the other person.

1　**Closed question**—Are there any openings in your company?

　　Open question—Have you hired anyone with my background in the past year? What do the hiring trends look like over the next six months to one year at your company?

2　**Closed question**—Joe gave me your name and said you might be able to put me in touch with a hiring manager or HR person in your company.

　　Open question -I was speaking with Joe and he said that you are very well-informed and well-connected in the telecommunications industry. I am presently researching your industry and was wondering if you have time to answer some questions and share your knowledge and expertise?

4　**Closed question**—Do you know anyone else that hires?

　　Open question—Who else would you recommend that I speak with to help me with my research in the industry? (Further prompt question is: Is there anyone else you can think of?)

Although asking questions is the first step in this exchange of information, you must also be willing to share information and help and support others along the way. When you engage people in an exchange of information, you might be led in directions that you would have never thought of on your own. This might also be true for the person you are exchanging the information with.

Networking is about developing a core group of people who you can help and can help you along your career path—Career Friendships

Janet, Karen and Samantha met over 20 years ago at the beginning of their careers. Although the three have only worked together twice over that period, their careers have remained intertwined. For instance, when Janet and Karen owned a business together for a number of years and had to close it down, Samantha helped Janet land a position at the company where she was working. Years later, when Samantha wanted to change companies, Karen helped Samantha secure a position at another organization.

During each of these moves over the past twenty years, the women have assisted each other in some way. Every three months they have dinner together to catch up on their personal and career lives. They exchange information, offer career support to each other and are always willing to work their perspective networks when one or the other has been downsized. They do not socialize with each other's families often, yet their friendship and support of one another is solid. "After my husband, they are among the first people I share news with about the ups and downs of my career and business. I know that I can count on them for help if I am ever out of work. Their support is part of my career safety net," Samantha explains.

It is important to remember that your networks do not have to be large or particularly influential. Remember what we said earlier about *six degrees of separation*. Everybody knows somebody and it is important to maintain those professional relationships. We are now working in a corporate environment that has a *'turnstile'* approach to its management and employees. Downsizing is moving at the speed of light.

In the old style workplace, you stayed with a company for years and you knew the management. People that moved around were considered unstable. In the present corporate environment, the continuous movement of employees makes it easy to lose track of where people have gone. One of the biggest problems individuals face in the workplace is tracking former managers for references.

Josie was recently downsized from a large utilities firm eight months after her boss of six years was laid off. "I was about to receive an offer for a great position within a new industry. All I needed was to track down my former boss. The company I was applying to would not accept the person I had worked with for the last eight months as a reference. The problem was that after my boss left the company, I felt so bad and guilty that I did not call him. Then, when I tried to locate him, he had moved and no one knew where to find him."

Josie is like many people. She feels guilty about keeping her job during a downsizing while others walk through the door to the unknown. Instead of starting what is perceived as an uncomfortable conversation with the person who has left the company, she will not call. The lesson is to keep track of former managers and co-workers because they can be excellent individuals to network with. As they go off and find other positions, they can also be key players in helping you land your next job. If you cannot locate these people, you may lose out on an opportunity because you do not have the proper references.

Networking is about investing in future possibilities.

Networking is the key to survival and success in any business, including your career. It is a skill you need to invest in. That may mean attending workshops, reading books and investing your own money to acquire the proper tools to build a network.

Some of the best networkers in the world are salespeople. The key reason is that one basic sales technique is referral marketing. Networking helps you gain access to information, move from one position to another and increase your knowledge and expertise. Therefore, you need to develop a style and a comfort level that suits you. This can be done by gaining as much information and knowledge on networking as possible so that you can learn this skill. You may never love or even be completely comfortable being a networker, but it is a must in career management.

10+1 Ways to Overcome Your Fear of Networking

1 Start with a safe zone—your friends, family and co-workers. When asking friends to help you move forward, remember that one day you will have the opportunity to help them because the average position only lasts 2.5 years.

2 Start with a letter, note or e-mail of introduction combined with a follow-up call.

3 Make your networking calls when your energy is at its peak. Stand up and have a mirror in front of you.

4 Prepare a script and practice before making the call. Use a tape recorder or leave a message on your own voice mail.

5 Know the purpose of your call. Write it down and look at it during the conversation. Don't waste your time or that of the other person with idle conversation about current issues or the person who introduced you.

6 Have a goal of introducing yourself via phone, events or e-mail at least once a day for ten days at the beginning of your networking learning journey.

7 Take the time to recharge your energy and plan your networking strategy. Know that the benefits outweigh the downside.

8 Get as much help from your friends as possible, especially if networking is not number one on your list of favorite things to do.

9 Breathe deeply for at least five minutes before you make a call if you are nervous.

10 After every call, ask what you can improve on or do differently the next time out. Never let a mistake or words that have not come out properly be the reason you give up on networking.

11 *Bonus*= Teach your children everything you know about networking so they never have to conquer the fear.

When you combine your ideas with others, you also increase your collective experience and knowledge. You cannot possibly know all there is to know. Strategic partnering adds other people's experience and knowledge with yours to increase your library.

Exercise

- Think of somebody you know (it can be anybody) and ask him or her to help you come up with three ideas to help you overcome some of the obstacles you face in your career. Ask him or her for any experiences or contacts that might help you.

- Now turn around and help that person develop three ideas to help him or her with his or her career challenges. Give your experiences or contacts to him or her.

Flexible Thinker Tool #3
Library

Where can you use your own library of experiences and knowledge to help you overcome your obstacles? Do you block other people's knowledge by quickly saying 'no' to their library? How do you double your library within seconds? Ask somebody for his or her library.

Both companies and people do networking. By having a broad network of people, you are able to build on their knowledge, experiences and contacts to secure your next opportunity.

Ultimately, the more you know the more flexible you will be and the greater career success you will enjoy. Constantly expand your knowledge by building your skills, reading, learning, and networking. In our economy, the person with the greatest **Library** will be the one who is always in demand in the job market.

Get *Networking* Educated

Tony had dreamed of being a firefighter from the time he was 12 years old. "Our next door neighbor was a firefighter and every time his pager went off his daughter would call me and I would run to the fire department and chase the fire trucks." At the age of 18, Tony was determined to fulfill his dream of being a firefighter. As time passed, the hiring process discouraged him and the need to find employment compelled Tony to take a position in construction.

As the years went by and Tony's career in construction soared, his dream of being a firefighter died. "I wanted to keep a piece of my dream so I volunteered as a firefighter in the small town I lived in. Eventually, I became a senior volunteer firefighter. I loved every minute of it, the hands-on learning, helping people, the rush of firefighting. As the years passed by, I became so involved that I got to know fire chiefs, the firefighters themselves, and everyone associated with the firefighting business in surrounding cities."

While he was ordering equipment for the fire department he volunteered for, a salesperson told Tony of a fire chief position that was available in a town approximately two hours away from where he had lived all his life. The salesperson felt that Tony would be perfect for the position.

At first Tony was apprehensive, and not really convinced that he had a shot at the position, but he went ahead and applied anyway. Using all his contacts, he secured an interview and references. Eighteen years after his initial attempt, Tony was offered the position of fire chief. "It was not an easy decision. The pay was $30,000 less than what I was making and it meant a move for my family. It was, however, a dream come true so I decided to take it. I know that it would never have happened without my volunteer experience and the networking contacts I made over the years while volunteering."

Volunteering is just one of many ways to increase your networking and find employment. Volunteering can also help you gain the skills and experience that are necessary to change careers. Tony is one of many people who have used the volunteer network route to secure a dream job.

Networking is both a skill and an art that requires time and effort. The following are some of the ways you can expand and increase your networking skills:

- Attend workshops and training sessions on networking. Don't forget to keep a list of the names of everyone who attended the session.
- Write down the names of everyone you know and take the time to keep in touch. E-mail is a great time saver.
- Join networking groups.
- Become a member of industry associations, business networking groups, rotary clubs, etc.
- Volunteer!
- Research e-networking groups or start one of your own.
- Phone people you previously worked with just to say hi. Never lose touch with the people you have worked with!
- Join former corporate alumni groups.
- Help people along the way. The individual who is great at networking is always willing to give out more information than they will ever receive.

The Eight Deadly Sins of Networking[1] by Max Messmer

1 Making promises you know you are incapable of keeping.

2 Making promises you're capable of keeping but failing to keep them.

3 Having a hidden agenda. For example, you call someone and announce you have a question you want answered when what you really want is a favor.

4 Using someone's name as a door opener without first clearing it with the person whose name you are using.

5 Not being considerate—that is not taking into account when you ask someone for help how difficult it may be for them to provide that help and being resentful when they don't respond quickly enough.

---

[1] Max Messmer, Managing Your Career for Dummies (John Wiley & Sons, 2000).

6   Discussing business at inappropriate times, such as at a wedding or sports event where the other person may be doing his best to forget about business.

7   Not showing your appreciation (a phone call or card) when someone has done you a favor.

8   Putting persistent pressure on people who've agreed to help you.

Step Two—*Target Marketing*

Kelly had been downsized from her position as vice president of human resources for a global technical firm. She decided that this was her opportunity to break out of the technical industry and into something completely different. When she was younger, she had worked at an insurance company and decided that that industry would be ideal as one of her target industries. Kelly had identified one insurance company in particular that she was interested in. She did not, however, have a contact and was hesitant to make a cold call to the company. Kelly met with her consultant and explained her dilemma. The consultant also agreed that making a cold call would not be as effective as having an introduction of some kind. The consultant remembered an article that she had read in a business magazine about the CEO of one of the top insurance companies and suggested that Kelly write a note congratulating him on the article and his success.

In the note, Kelly also explained that she was targeting the insurance industry in a job search and requested the name of an individual in the company that could answer questions about the industry and how best to approach opportunities in the future. The response was incredible to say the least. The CEO passed the information along to a senior executive in the company who not only called Kelly, but also invited her out to lunch at the request of the CEO.

Kelly met with the executive and had a very informative lunch. Although there were no positions available at Kelly's level, the two agreed to stay in touch over the next few months. Kelly ended up accepting a position back at her old company, but she continued to stay in touch with the executive at the insurance company and now considers her as part of her network.

Getting Creative
The following is a list of creative ways to target market specific companies and industries.

Put your feet up on the desk and read the newspaper.

Read the newspaper and business magazines everyday.

Newspapers and business magazines provide a wealth of information on movement in the business marketplace. During a job search, most people relate the newspaper specifically to the want ads. The financial and business sections, however, are the places to be cruising when you are involved in a job search. The financial section can provide you with names and information about companies and industries that are growing and doing well financially. The business section can give you insight into new market trends and very specific information about the development of new products and services that are emerging in the marketplace. You can then take this information and target companies and people that are featured in the articles.

Send a handwritten note or make a phone call to the person featured in the article telling them how much you enjoyed the information.

The next step is to take the information that you are gathering from articles and use that information to connect with the company or the person featured in the article. This is what Kelly did in the story at the beginning of this section. Would it not be better to target a company for a specific reason instead of making a complete cold call? By sending a note first and then following up with a phone call, you have created a great starting point and ice breaker for a conversation that focuses on the company and/or person in the article. The majority of individuals and companies that are featured in articles like to be recognized and have their information acknowledged. The editors of the newspaper sections will always forward your e-mail to the person or company that was written about.

Send a handwritten note or make a phone call offering congratulations to individuals who have just been recently promoted.

Everyday in newspapers across North America companies announce senior management promotions and hires. This is a wonderful opportunity to start a conversation with a person that you do not know. When people start a new position they are usually not yet fully entrenched in the work that is before them, so they may have more time to talk and think about hiring and bringing their own people on board. Oftentimes, with new leadership, changes are just around the corner. You can ask that person about the hiring process, what his or her approach was, and so on. People love to talk about their successes.

Research and watch out for industries that are in a growth mode. Target today for tomorrow's job or career.

Reading newspapers and magazines on a regular basis is a great way to track and watch out for industries that are in growth mode. For instance, Michael, an aerospace engineer, believes he needs to make a change because his industry is shrinking. Last year while still working, he hired a career management coach and was directed to start following new industry trends and growth.

After coming across an article on windmill power and technology, Michael wrote a note to follow up with the company. He was directed to a contact in the engineering department who was happy to share information. Although the company was small and there is not a huge demand for windmill technology as yet, the future was certainly looking bright.

Michael exchanged several phone calls and e-mails with the engineer. The engineer gave Michael advice on where to get additional information and what books to read on the technology. He was helping Michael prepare for future opportunities within the wind power industry. Although the company was not presently hiring, Michael felt assured that if a position became available the engineer would have no problem referring him.

Michael is building a network for the future by keeping an eye on trends in the marketplace today. If you are looking to make a career change, be prepared for the fact that this may not happen overnight or on your first attempt. You may need to go back to school to acquire additional skills. Even a degree (if required) does not necessarily mean that you can jump into a new industry. It is important to target these industries ahead of time to make contacts for future possibilities. There are many great books that discuss future trends and career possibilities and we recommend that you explore them.

Every Dream is a Job

Lisa is 35 years old and has been working in the telecommunications industry as a sales and marketing professional for the past ten years. Although she has been very successful and is still employed, she believes that she has to prepare for a plan B because of the large number of downsizes within her company and the industry in general. She knows that that may mean a career change.

Lisa was given an assignment where she had to come up with approximately five industries that she could start to research and network in immediately. The idea behind this was not just to choose the obvious, but also to choose a few industries completely outside the telecommunications industry, the same way Michael did with the windmill technology. She was encouraged to list a 'dream' industry, even if it seemed 'out of reach' and not practical at the time.

First of all, Lisa chose telecommunications because this is her area of expertise where she has had many successes. Next she chose technology services because Lisa believed that she would be able to easily transfer her skills selling and marketing telecommunication systems and services into selling any number of technology services. Her third choice was the staffing industry. Again, this industry is service-based and is in growth mode. Also, many of the large agencies are national in scope. Lisa has a friend who has been very successful in the industry and has already discussed career possibilities with her. A position in this industry would also play to her strong sales and marketing background.

Finally, Lisa decided to check out the golf industry. Lisa loves to play golf so this is her dream industry. In addition, she recently read the book *Boom, Bust and Echo* by David Foote and learned that golf is one of the fastest growing sports industries for baby boomers. Lisa is not sure how her background will apply, but wants to start the research for future possibilities.

Lisa was then instructed by her career coach to research approximately 10 companies or more for each industry. She was also told to read any articles that had been written about the industry or specific companies within the industries she had selected. When she completed her assignment, she was then instructed to start using the networking process to get contacts within her selected industries and companies.

What really excited Lisa was that she found out that there is a huge demand for people to sell golf tournaments to corporations for social and charity events. Lisa felt that with her contacts, this could definitely be a future possibility.

How to Decide on Your Target Markets

What Lisa did was to target market. She decided on the industries or companies that most interested her. Then she increased her knowledge and her network in that target market. This prepared her for loss of employment in the future. Even though Lisa ultimately decided to stay with her company, she became much more flexible because she created options. The more options you have, the more flexible you are. If Lisa decides later to leave her company, she will be prepared to make a complete career shift and develop a position outside her current industry.

Step Three—Partnering with Recruiters

Important Career Tip—Partner with recruiters throughout the lifetime of your career.

Regardless of your past experiences, the facts speak for themselves!

- ➤ The recruitment industry is a multi-billion-dollar industry.
- ➤ The number one staffing service achieved approximately 18 billion in sales last year.
- ➤ Every one of the Fortune 100 companies has used staffing services over the last five years.
- ➤ In 2002, the top employer was not Ford or GM, but Manpower. In 2003, it was Adecco.
- ➤ Thirty-eight percent of all contract/temporary positions become full-time.

If the above information is not enough to compel you to seek out a recruiter, then think about the fact that 25 to 30 percent of all positions are in the hands of recruiters, while only 5 percent of positions come from the Internet.

To successfully build a relationship with a recruiter, you first need to understand the staffing industry and the role of the recruiter. This information relates directly to your career. The following questions are those most asked by our clients during workshops and coaching sessions. They were also put to recruiters currently working in the staffing industry. The answers are a compilation of the recruiters' responses and will help you understand how to successfully navigate through the world of recruiters and build a career relationship with them.

What is the role of a recruiter in my job search?

Finding the right recruiter that specializes in your industry is not easy. A recruiter's role is not to find jobs for people, but to fill positions for their paying clients. The client gives the recruiter a job description and his/her role is to match the qualifications the client has identified with the culture and environment to make a successful match. In an applicant tight market (a market where there are more positions than applicants), recruiters can give the mistaken impression that they are trying to help people find jobs. The reason for this is that they are calling upon potential applicants and presenting them with job opportunities since there are not enough applicants applying for job postings or available to fill their orders. As a result, recruiters become more proactive in their search process.

When the market turns to an employers' market however, the tables turn. Recruiters are not as accessible and they can give the impression that they have no interest in helping applicants. This happens because they have too many people applying for positions and a large applicant pool to choose from. Like everyone else in business they have a role to play. Their bottom line is that they fill the orders that are given to them by the paying client.

Why do recruiters never respond to my phone calls or e-mails?

This normally takes place when there is an abundance of applicants and a shortage of positions available. Many of the recruiters also explained that technology has completely changed how they do their job. It used to be that resumés where sent by mail and/or fax. Now that e-mail has become a way of life, it has increased responses to the point where it is impossible for a recruiter to return phone calls or respond to e-mails. The average recruiter gets approximately 200 responses to a job posting in a market where there is a job shortage. This makes it physically impossible to respond to everybody. Many of the recruiters we spoke to wish that they could do a better of job of communicating this. Their only recourse, however, is to state on a job posting that only the applicants chosen will be contacted. You should also note that your resumé is being entered into a resumé retrieval system that will be there for future opportunities.

How often should I contact/follow up with a recruiter after I submit my resumé?

Follow-up is a crucial part of the job search process and should be done in a professional manner without a trace of frustration in your voice. Applicants applying for positions can risk the opposite effect. This is jokingly called stalking—when an applicant is calling everyday and, in some cases, more than once a day.

The frustrating part for many applicants is that when they apply for a position, they have no name with which to follow up. That is why it is important to use networking techniques to connect with recruiters. Many of the recruiters that we spoke to explained that in many cases a professional follow-up phone call has prompted the recruiter to seek out the resumé and call the applicant. On the other hand, a voice mail or phone call that is aggressive or filled with anger has caused the recruiter to completely eliminate a potential candidate.

Follow-up should be made within 24 hours after the resumé is submitted. Subsequent follow-up should be made anywhere from one to two weeks after. You can also discuss this with the recruiter and find out what he or she is comfortable with. The better the relationship you have with a recruiter, the easier it is to pick up the phone and have a conversation.

For more information on making a professional follow-up call, see pp. 103.

How many recruiters should I register with at one time?

Many people are advised to only use a few recruiters at a time. The challenge with this advice is that when you submit your resumé in response to a position posted on an agency web site, it does not mean that you are registered. Registered means that you have had a face-to-face interview or, in some cases, a phone interview so that the recruiter has knowledge of your background and circumstances.

Remember, this is your career and your livelihood. Limiting yourself to one or two recruiters will limit the opportunities that will be available to you. The best approach is to research all the agencies that recruit in your field of expertise and/or where the location is suitable to you. You can then apply to the recruiters that meet your specific criteria. This may mean 15 to 20 different agencies. In no way will you have relationships with all of them. What will happen is that many will not have suitable positions, some may not even return calls, or you may find that there is no connection between you and the recruiter.

You can then narrow the number down to four or five that are suitable. In a market where there are few jobs and many applicants, recruiters will want you to look to other resources. This is because they do not want the burden of potential applicants depending on them to find employment. When the market is the reverse—few applicants and many job openings—a recruiter may immediately recognize that s/he can find you a position and ask that you not go to other recruiters. This may be very complimentary. However, you risk limiting your range of opportunities. If you feel compelled to agree to use only one recruiter at a time, give the recruiter a time limit from a few days to one week so that you can be sure s/he is able to secure interviews for you. If you decide not to be exclusive, explain your wish to pursue relationships with other recruiters. Don't worry too much about the consequences. If you are that marketable, the recruiter will still work hard to make the placement. After all, that is how recruiters earn their livelihoods.

In what way will a recruiter benefit my career?

If you build the relationships and partner with recruiters throughout the lifetime of your career, a recruiter can, over the years, benefit your career in many ways. Recruiters have their fingers on the pulse of the marketplace. They know who is hiring and who is not. They are also aware of what processes, technical skills and soft skills are currently in demand. Recruiters can also give you advice on how to improve your resumé and conduct yourself in an interview. They are very knowledgeable about the companies they recruit for. After all, it is their job.

If you foster relationships with recruiters and keep in touch with them, they can give you advice on skills or the knowledge that you will need to stay marketable. If you are working, keep in touch with recruiters so that they can let you know about opportunities that are on the horizon.

When a recruiter calls, you should take the time to listen, even if the position being presented is not for you. Try to recommend a friend or someone you may have worked with. Many people we talk to take offence when a recruiter calls while they are working. We believe, however, it is an opportunity for you to build relationships. After all, you never know when your company may be downsizing or reorganizing.

How does a recruiter get paid, and do recruiters only care about their commission cheque?

Recently, we held a three-day workshop for a group of individuals who were downsized from a telecommunications company. One of the presenters at that workshop was a seasoned veteran of the staffing industry. She was currently the branch manager with one of the key players in the industry. Doris was there to discuss the staffing industry and how to successfully navigate through the many different types of agencies. After her presentation, she opened the floor for questions and impressions.

The mood that day was not good. Many of the individuals attending the workshop saw Doris's presence as an opportunity to vent their frustrations about the staffing industry. One participant got right to the point within 15 minutes of the presentation. His comment was, "Recruiters only care about the bottom line and their commission cheques. It's just about money." Everyone in the room nodded in agreement.

Doris walked to the middle of the u-shaped conference table and looked around the room at each participant. She then asked this question, "If one person in this room can tell me that the company they previously worked for did not care about the bottom line, I will concede that you are correct and walk out the door."

Not one person answered. They all looked at each other and finally one person laughed. He then turned to the group and said, "The reason we are here is because of the bottom line." With that, everyone laughed as well and nodded their heads in agreement. Doris went on to explain that yes the staffing industry was sales and profit focused. If she did not meet the financial objectives required by her company, she too would be looking for employment. Like every other business, however, they had to take the big picture into account when doing day-to-day business.

A recruiter has more to lose than money when something goes wrong with a placement. Recruiters become successful based on their reputation and ability to do a good job. For example if a recruiter places an applicant with a client company and that person stays with the company and becomes successful, the client company will give the recruiter repeat business because they know from past experience that the recruiter understands their corporate culture and key requirements. In turn, the applicant that was placed in the position will feel a sense of loyalty to the recruiter. When and if s/he is in a position to hire, his/her most likely choice will be the recruiter that placed him/her in that position. On the other side of the coin, if the recruiter places a candidate that does not work out, the recruiter will have to replace that person or give back the fee that was paid by the company for the search. The company and applicant will both feel disappointed by the results and it can severely hurt the recruiters' reputation. This bad taste may even lead to the loss of future business.

Many of the large recruitment firms pay their recruiters a base salary plus bonus or commission. This commission/bonus is based on individual, branch, or team performance. There are many recruiters out there that work strictly on commission. The stakes are high if they do not perform, but the rewards are equally high if they do.

The real bottom line is that when you are conducting a job search you should not concern yourself with how recruiters get paid. Instead, the focus should be on the quality of the service and how that recruiter can benefit you and your job search.

How do you know if a recruiter is reputable?

People always ask for the name of a good recruiter or staffing service. Like any professional service, there are good and bad providers. It is up to you to seek out recruiters and develop the relationship. The foundation to a good relationship or partnership is built over time. Having said that, the number one way to get connected to a recruiter is to be referred by someone you know.

There is no difference between networking with other people to find an opportunity for yourself and networking to find a recruiter in your industry. Go back to the networking section of this book and use the techniques for networking to get names and introductions.

Another good technique is to speak to managers and human resources professionals and ask them what companies they use to recruit staff. It is significantly easier to phone a recruiter and say, "I have been referred to you by Bob Smith at ABC Corporation" than to simply make a cold call. A recruiter will want to please a corporate client and, if s/he is smart, the recruiter will take the time to speak with you. For individuals who have recently been downsized or left a company, go back to the corporation that you were previously working for (if you have a positive relationship) and ask for the names of recruiters that they are currently working with. Another approach is to ask the human resources person or manager to call the recruiters ahead of time as a way to introduce you to them.

What is the difference between a contingency and retainer recruiter?

- *Contingency.* Most staffing services work on a contingency basis. That means that the agency that fills the order bills the client. You may notice when you are searching for positions on the Internet that many positions posted with different agencies are very similar. That is because corporations will give the job description/order to several agencies at one time. This ensures that the order is filled with the best-qualified candidate quickly. Most organizations will not depend on one service to fill their job orders. The competition can be fierce because no matter how much work a recruiter does (i.e. advertising/posting, interviewing, reference checking, presenting candidates, etc.) or the money they spend on a search, they receive no compensation if they do not present a candidate that gets hired.

- *Retainer.* Very few services work on retainer. Most of these services fill executive or very specialized positions. The agency may have to invest a considerable amount of money to locate the right candidate (i.e. travel and meeting expenses). The agency is paid one-third up front for the search to begin, one-third when the candidates are presented and the final amount when the candidate starts the job. This will most likely be an exclusive search for the agency. If for some reason the organization does not hire anybody, the money that was paid in advance is still kept by the agency.

Why can't I go around the recruiter to the corporate client if the search process is too slow and I am familiar with the company?

Christine had worked very hard with her career management coach. Together they created a resumé that was in line with the marketplace, learned important interviewing skills and implemented a work search action plan. Christine was starting to see her hard work resulting in interviews. One of the most promising of these came from a recruiter who introduced her to a pharmaceutical company that was in search of a person with Christine's background. Christine was chosen as one of the lucky candidates for the first round of interviews. The interview went well and the HR person said that she would definitely request that Christine come back for a second interview. Immediately after the interview, the recruiter explained that he had just spoken to the HR person at the pharmaceutical company and confirmed that Christine would have a second interview, but it would take approximately one week to set up.

Christine anxiously waited and when she did not hear back from the recruiter at the end of the week, she called and left a message. She continued to call and leave messages over the next week and a half but did not get a return call. At one point, the receptionist at the agency explained that the recruiter was a very busy person. In frustration, she phoned her career management coach and asked her what harm it would do if she followed up with the HR person at the client company herself.

The career coach explained that if she did go directly to the company, she would risk being dismissed as a candidate for the job by both the recruiter and the HR person. Here are some reasons why you should never circumvent a recruiter who has sent you on a job interview:

- You are not following protocol and risk giving the impression that you do not know how to follow simple procedures. Many companies shy away from individuals that are lone rangers and work outside the system. The company had given the job order to the recruiter and was willing to pay a large amount of money for the service so that they did not have to directly manage the calls, e-mails, etc. If they wanted to hire directly, they would not have engaged a recruiter to help them find a suitable candidate.
- You risk incurring the wrath of the recruiter for circumventing his/her authority and management of the process. This could easily lead to you losing not only this opportunity, but future opportunities with the agency and maybe other staffing services as well.

After pointing out all this information to Christine, the career management coach agreed that the recruiter did owe Christine a follow-up call regardless of the result of her interview. She had every right to be frustrated by the recruiter's unprofessional behavior. The coach offered her a completely different solution. Christine was to call the recruiter and leave the following message:

"I understand from your receptionist and after leaving a number of messages that you are very busy! I do not want to bother you so I have decided to phone the client and follow up about the second interview to see if I am still being considered. I will wait until tomorrow to do this just in case you have other information for me. If I do not hear from you by then, I will assume that you want me to go ahead and call your client."

The recruiter was on the phone to Christine within a half-hour explaining that the client's child had taken ill so she has not been in the office but was due to return the following week. He also apologized that he had taken so long to follow up and explained that it is never a good idea to call a client. Christine thanked him, knowing that she had got the result she desired.

Getting angry with a recruiter in this kind of situation will never work in your favor. Therefore, finding creative ways to get the results you want (like Christine did) is a better approach.

Are the positions that recruiters post real?

Over the years we have been asked this question constantly. Many individuals feel that recruiters post positions that are not real in order to add potential applicants to their data banks.

The first thing you need to know is that it is illegal for any organization, not just staffing services, to post positions that are not available. If any company was questioned on this they would have to provide documentation to prove the legitimacy of the position. For instance, staffing services would have to show the name of the company and the name of the individual who released the job order to the recruiter.

In spite of the legalities, there is still a perception that postings on the Internet that are there for months do not get replies from potential applicants. When we questioned recruiters about this in our survey, they explained a number of reasons why this happens and why they also find the situation annoying.

- Recruiters notify the job boards when the order is filled. Recruiters, however, are at the mercy of the job boards' technical staff or their own in-house staff to remove the positions posted and this sometimes can be a long process.

- Most recruiters agreed that in some cases, especially when there is an applicant tight market, positions can be left to linger because they may attract candidates for other positions the recruiter is working on.

- Another reason cited is that the job boards want to create the impression for their advertisers and potential advertisers that there is a lot of traffic that will attract people viewing advertisements.

- All recruiters agreed that when it is an employers' market, positions left on the job boards become nothing but a nuisance with potential candidates constantly calling and emailing resumés. The recruiters all said that this is a very irritating part of the job because it is impossible for them to manage the enormous amount of correspondence.

One other thing to watch out for is general ads posted on job boards that clearly state the staffing service is looking to build their resumé database. An example of this kind of ad might be:

General laborers with two years experience and work boots needed for a variety of positions in the downtown area. Or, Cobol programmers willing to travel across Canada and the U.S. needed to work on short-term projects

The following is a list of the most successful ways to attract a recruiter's attention:

The Recruiter's Directory

Most job boards will have a link to a recruiter's directories and/or to the various recruiters' associations which can also lead you to a recruiter's directory in your area. Most of these directories are under $100 and should be part of your career management tool kit. This is an investment you will need to make on your own with your own money.

Most of the directories break down staffing services by industries, professions and locations that they recruit in. Here are a couple of examples of directory listings.

ABC Recruitment Service specializing in sales and marketing positions for the downtown core.

Smith & Douglas Recruiters specializing in recruiting for the pharmaceutical industry across North America.

Many staffing services can recruit for positions across the board—administrative, management, sales and light industrial. For specific areas, however, you may have to find different recruiters who look after a specific industry or profession.

Persistence/Follow-up

As we said earlier, most of the recruiters explained to us that a professional follow-up call can inspire them to search for a resumé and review it. A person with a professional voice and manner can stand out in a crowd of hundreds. The reverse of that, however, is also true. The individual who calls complaining about the process or becomes a stalker by constantly calling the recruiter and leaving messages may cause the recruiter to eliminate the candidate.

Here is an example of a professional message:

Hello Katie, my name is Joanne Bell and I am following up to first see if you received my resumé for the position you posted on April 2nd for a marketing manager for a sports retail company. I would also like to find out if you are considering my 10 years of experience in a similar retail industry and if not, wondered if you would keep my resumé on file for future searches. I can be reached at (124) 456-7890 and would love the opportunity to speak with you.

The opposite approach may sound like this:

Hello Katie, my name is Shelia Cote. I sent my resumé to you for the marketing manager position for a sports retail company. I have not heard back and it has been two weeks. I am extremely disappointed with your response. As you know, I have the experience you are looking for based on the posting. I am waiting for your call and my number is (123) 109-8787.

Many people assume that they can say things to recruiters that they would never say to a hiring manager or human resources professional at the company they are applying to for employment. Never make that mistake. A recruiter has the power to make the decision as to whose resumé they will send to a company for a specific position. Remember, the company gave the recruiter the power to make that decision.

The ideal time to place a follow-up call is one to two days after you have e-mailed your resumé. Continue to call and leave a professional message once or twice a week. You can also send an e-mail within the first three weeks of the posting. If you have still not received a response, you may want to continue to try to get feedback as to why you were not chosen. Call once every second week if you really want to speak with the recruiter for other positions. When you have made contact with the recruiter, ask his/her opinion on an acceptable timeframe for the follow-up process.

In real estate there is a well-known saying, "Location, location, location." We believe that in the job search process the saying is, "Follow up, follow up, and follow up." We know what you are thinking. Are there times when it is impossible to find out the name of the recruiter or to get through to the recruiter? Yes, that is true. However, that is also when you have to become flexible. Network your way in to overcome the obstacle you may face. We agree that there are dead ends. But, you must not let them serve as benchmarks for every position, nor the reason why you do not attempt a full follow-up process.

Sharing industry knowledge and exchanging information with a recruiter.

Many of the participants in our workshops tell us stories about how recruiters used to call them when they were working at their former companies during times when the job market was really hot. When we ask these people if they listened to the recruiter or made any referrals, most of them reply that they were too busy to talk to the recruiter or that they were not interested since they were happy with their current positions. Others simply felt it was disloyal to the company and some even expressed anger at the recruiter for daring to call them while they were working. Since many of the people in our workshops have been downsized, we always ask the question, "What would it be like now if you had listened to that recruiter, developed a relationship, exchanged information or even given him/her the name of a person who might have been interested?" Their reply is usually that they would now have a contact that they could call.

Most people only think of recruiters when they are looking for a position, not while they are working. This mindset has to change. Most of us have a working relationship with a doctor, lawyer and other professionals even though we are not constantly in need of their services on a regular basis. Why not have working relationships with a few recruiters so we are prepared when the need arises? If the average job in North America now only lasts 2.5 years, it is wise to have a recruiter close at hand for the times when we are looking for a new opportunity.

If you have recently found employment, a good strategy is to send a thank you note, e-mail or call informing the recruiter of your new position and thanking him/her for any assistance s/he may have given you. Also note that when you are settled in, you will call him/her with further details. If you found a recruiter especially helpful, you may want to introduce that person to the HR department of your new company. By doing this, you are continuing the relationship and spreading goodwill. This will pay off in the long term. You must also remember to send recruiters an updated copy of your resumé every six months to a year.

Referrals

Referrals mean networking and this is the number one way to attract a recruiter's attention. The best approach is to ask everyone you know what recruiters they have used and then get referrals. If you have been recently downsized, go back to the HR department of the company you worked for and ask for a referral to the recruitment firm the company is presently using. The recruiter is not going to ignore a referral from a client company and most recruiters believe in the old adage, "Good people know good people."

Reread the networking section and apply those techniques to gathering referrals and introductions to recruiters. This is a much easier approach than making constant cold calls.

Associations/Alumni

It is fair to say that for every industry, profession, trade, etc. you will find a recruiter/staffing service that specializes in recruitment for that particular market. If your industry or profession has an association and has monthly, quarterly or yearly events, the chances are that you will also find a recruiter attending these events. Why?!? Because it is part of a recruiter's job to be out there in the community attending the association events of their clients and potential applicants. This type of event give recruiters exposure, networking opportunities and the opportunity to meet clients who they otherwise might never even have a phone conversation with.

Wouldn't it be easier to approach recruiters in person, introduce yourself and get their cards at one of these events instead of trying to make a cold call? You can also call your association and ask for the names of recruiters that are members or are listed as attendees. Recruiters will also post jobs on the web sites of associations.

Many people drop their association memberships after they have been downsized from a company because of cost. You may want to negotiate into your package that the company continues to pay your membership fees for the next six months or until you are employed. Associations are a good investment and you should seriously consider paying for the membership on your own if the company you work for will not consider it. Association meetings can give you the opportunity to network in a focused way. One of our clients sat on the board of three different associations and considered this his number one source for finding employment, as well as a great way to promote himself within his industry. In fact, he credits his association memberships with helping him secure three positions over the last ten years. Each opportunity came from people he met through the associations.

Corporate alumni associations are now popping up all across North America. Companies realize that downsizing today could mean hiring tomorrow and want to track where their employees can be found. Alumni web sites allow corporations to pull potential candidates as they need them. On some sites, recruiters and organizations are also allowed to advertise opportunities that are available. These sites are a great way to network and get important information. If your former company has an alumni site, it is recommended that you stay active on it, if only to keep track of your references.

Recruiters are also a great source of industry information. Because of their relationships with organizations, they always have their fingers on the pulse of the marketplace. Recruiters know who is hiring, where the latest trends are, and the markets that are not doing well.

Step Four—*The Internet*

- Post your resumé on as many job sites/boards that are relevant to the position you are seeking.

- Remember to keep track of where your resumé is posted and what types of positions you applied for.

- The Internet represents only 5 percent of the positions available. Do not risk spending 80 percent of your time in a place that produces only 5 percent of the results.

Once you have posted your information, you need to maintain and track it. Do not, however, make this the focus of your day if you are presently looking for employment.

WARNING

Individuals who spend all their time on the Internet risk becoming islands unto themselves. In a real world sense, they are simply putting a message in a bottle and throwing it into a vast sea, hoping that someone answers!

The Action Plan

You know that you need to network, meet with recruiters, target market and post your resumé on the Internet. Now the question is, how do you manage to combine these tasks and still stay accountable to yourself? How do you know if you are on the right track? How do you organize your day if you are looking for a position full-time? Most people find it a daunting task to start the implementation process. Many get stuck at the resumé posting stage and some find that their days are wasted on chores around the house. Others spend endless unproductive hours on research and organization.

In a work environment, we can give the same people a project with goals and accountabilities and they will easily accomplish the end result by applying a system. When you are working, it is important to effectively organize your work hours and fully utilize the resources available to you. It is the same with a work search. You should organize a work search campaign in the same way that you would any project you are required to complete.

When researching this book, we discovered one thing that was common to most of the career management programs and services on the market. They all emphasized the effectiveness of networking, target marketing, recruiters and the Internet. In some cases, the information they provided on networking and target marketing was excellent. However, the problem is that they did not go beyond this to outline an effective plan for implementing the process of finding a new position.

The work search action plan we have created has been tested on hundreds of people and its effectiveness is proven. The plan creates synergy and will provide you with a realistic and honest way to measure how you are spending your day. If you implement this very simple action plan, you will start to see the results within three weeks, including interviews, networking meetings, etc.

The following is a chart of the four areas that you will be focusing on during your work search action campaign.

- Spend at least one hour per day focusing on each of the four areas. This means that you will spend a minimum of four hours per day on your search.

WORK SEARCH ACTION PLAN

INTERNET	RECRUITERS	NETWORKING	TARGET MARKETING
Source of 5 percent of jobs	Source of 20 to 30 percent of jobs	Source of 60 percent of jobs	Combination
Post resumé on all job boards that are relevant to you.	Create a list of recruiters using the following techniques: 1. Referrals 2. Recruiter directories 3. Networking.	Create a list of networking contacts. Remember to double your list by asking each person for an additional contact.	Remember that target marketing is a combination of networking, the Internet and recruiters. Read magazines and newspapers. Pick four industries that you are interested in and then research 10 companies for each industry.

- The trick is to start your day with the area that you like the least, and finish your day with the area you like the most. *For example, if you hate networking and love the Internet, your day should be arranged in this order: networking, one hour; recruiters, one hour; target marketing, one hour; the Internet, one hour.* The only person you are hurting by cheating on this is you! By following this routine, you will give yourself something to look forward to at the end of the day and get the hard part out of the way at the beginning of the day.

- Create a *reverse critical path.* Start with the desired result and work backwards with the actions it will take to achieve those results. This becomes important when you need to have a position by a certain date. You must be realistic. Landing a management position can take three to six months. If it is February and you need to start a position by July 1st, you need to determine what the numbers are going to look like to get you to the interview and then break those numbers into stages so you reach your goal. Remember the sales campaign at the very beginning of this chapter that stated: *For every 100 brochures you send out you will be required to make 100 follow-up calls to create 10 face-to-face appointments that may land one sale.* You can be more certain of the numbers by researching the job market in your immediate area and/or profession and calculating from there. Also, remember that the interview stages take much longer in today's market with anywhere from three to six weeks being the new norm. This should be factored into the time it will take to land an offer.

- If you need to, go back and reread each of the four sections on marketing so you can fully understand and make the most of the techniques discussed in each section.

- Create a spreadsheet or system that will help you track the number of resumés you have posted, networking calls you have made and recruiters and companies you have contacted, etc. Have one column you can use to make notes about conversations and an additional column for follow-up information. *Remember that 50 resumés posted on the Internet with no contact does not equal or create the same results as having 50 networking conversations.*

- Keep your datebook at hand so you can also list the follow-up calls that you have committed to. This will help you keep a sense of purpose during each day.

- Results are measured by the number of networking conversations, meetings and interviews. Please note that when we say networking meetings we do not mean a conversation or coffee with a friend.

- Do a weekly review session. This will give you the opportunity to review how you can improve your networking.

In the networking section, we stated that a job search and sales campaign are similar because both are basically a numbers game. In other words, the more you put out there the more you will get back. When the action plan starts producing results it creates energy and excitement. It is amazing to watch people going from little action to massive action in a short period of time. When you start to see results

do not slow down on the four-hour minimum. That is because within two weeks you will be back at square one with few calls if any. Always remember that the ultimate goal is to land one to two offers!

At least once a week review your progress by asking yourself what is working and what is not. Immediately make changes and improvements. Ask people you feel comfortable with for feedback on your approach, resumé, etc. Never analyze a networking call immediately after you have made it. Just congratulate yourself for having done so.

It is important to take this action plan seriously. Work hard at the implementation and follow-up process. There may be times when you need to give yourself an afternoon or even a few days off for fun and relaxation. This is especially true if you are feeling frustrated and it is starting to show. The worst thing you can do during a job search is to let people in any way sense your fear and frustration.

If you do not have a career coach we highly recommend that you join a networking group or seek out an individual who is in a similar situation. This way you have somebody to check in with who can cheer you on and support you in times of frustration or disappointment.

Looking for a New Position while Working Full-time

Follow the work search action plan in the same way, but adjust your time frame accordingly. One way to do this is to spend one week on each of the four areas. For instance, one week you can post your resumé, the next week you can e-mail recruiters and follow up on your lunch hour. Some networking calls can be done during the day and you can always make time in the evening to put together a focused target marketing campaign.

If you apply the *4 Step Guide to Career Success* you will always be prepared for movement and not have to worry about looking for a position while you are working.

Chapter Six:

Presentation of Me Inc.
— The Interview

It is a fact that you project what you are.
NORMAN VINCENT PEALE

Bill had everything going for him. He was perfectly suited for his staffing industry position. After all, he had a solid background in sales, along with confidence, and lots of industry experience. He had worked for small boutique services and now wanted to take his career to the next level and work for one of the larger agencies. Securing an interview was easy. He was working with a recruiter who specialized in placement within the staffing industry and the recruiter had no problem getting Bill an interview with the largest global staffing service.

The recruiter warned Bill that this particular service had a tough interviewing process that included a number of interviews that were behavioral-based. They also did a series of evaluations to make sure the candidate fit in with the corporate culture. The company had a very strong succession planning process. This meant that applicants were evaluated not just on their ability to do the job, but also on their future potential.

It was suggested to Bill that he prepare carefully for the interview and spend time researching the company since his knowledge about the organization would be evaluated. Bill was very confident in his ability and his experience in the industry. So, he just quickly navigated through the company web site right before the interview. Neither was Bill too concerned about the interview process since he himself had been interviewing candidates for years and he had always been successful in securing positions because of his ability to develop relationships with people. After all, he was in sales.

Bill wanted this job. He knew that working with this company could offer the training and expertise that he needed in order to work his way up into an executive position in the future. When he arrived, he was introduced to the regional manager and her boss, the executive director of sales. Bill was not expecting to be interviewed by two people and was taken aback. It was quickly explained that the executive director had just happened to stop by the office because of a cancellation in her schedule that day and had decided to stay for the interview. It was explained to Bill that, if he were successful, he would have had to meet with her at another date anyway. So really, they were able to kill two birds with one stone by having the executive director there.

The interview started with the usual pleasantries. They talked about the industry in general and some networking connections they had in common. After 15 minutes, the regional manager started to review Bill's resumé. He was able to confidently speak to the reasons why he had moved from one company to the next and about some of his key learning experiences during the last few years. The director asked Bill what he knew about the company. Bill explained that he had reviewed the web site and was impressed by the many business units and the impressive sales of the company in the previous year.

The regional manager then asked what he thought about the company's recent acquisition of a competitor. Bill had no idea what she was talking about and honestly told her. The story had hit all the national papers. Both the regional manager and sales director expressed their surprise that Bill was not aware of this acquisition.

After a number of questions on a deeper level about the company and its direction, it became clear to Bill and the two interviewers that Bill had not done his homework. As the two jumped into the behavioral questioning portion of the interview, it was obvious to all in that room that Bill was out of his element and not prepared.

"They started asking questions such as, 'Give me an example of a time when a client had an issue with your ability to do the job and how you were able to deal with the client. Tell me about a time when you had successfully landed a sale for your company and at the last minute the customer changed the terms of the agreement and how you dealt with the situation. What was your number one accomplishment in the last year? What is the largest sale you made in the last year and how did that sale compare to those of the average salesperson in your company?' On and on they went. It was a nightmare. My mind went blank. I know I am good at my job. I was not, however, expecting this kind of detailed questioning. When I reflected the next day I realized that if I was prepared, I could have easily answered many of the questions. If only I had taken the time to review my sales numbers and my accomplishments, but it was too late."

When the recruiter that was dealing with Bill requested feedback on the interview from the regional manager, she was surprisingly candid about how things went. She explained that Bill was a nice guy but was better suited in her opinion to a smaller environment where the expectations were not so high. The manager explained that she was very disappointed in his lack of knowledge about the company. What that said to her was that Bill would not take the time to investigate and research potential clients, something the company felt was crucial in landing large accounts. Also, he had no sense of his own accomplishments and that told her that there was no depth to his overall business acumen. It seemed to her that he was just winging his career. The manager also explained that it used to be acceptable to just go in and build a relationship with a client based on a mutual consensus of liking each other. That, however, was no longer an acceptable way to do business. Instead a salesperson needs to be well versed in a potential client's businesses to anticipate future needs and provide the service needed on a long-term basis. It was also noted that Bill proceeded to get more and more nervous under pressure and that they were looking for people to work for them that knew how to recover in a pressure situation.

I Am Really Good at Winging It!
The Science of Interviewing in the 21st Century

Bill, like many who have had successful interviews in the past, feels that it is personality that gets the job. The playing field, however, has been leveled by stringent interviews that use a variety of techniques. Among these techniques are the behavioral interview and emotional intelligence evaluation. Winging it no longer works. You need to be prepared and demonstrate what it is that you can do for the company by explaining what you have done in the past.

The process has become very sophisticated due to the cost of hiring. In addition, there is the cost of loss of productivity if the person is not a proper fit and the organization has to start the process of hiring all over. Preparation is powerful. Most people will be nervous at the beginning of the interview, but if you are completely prepared, nerves will calm as you answer the questions and build a rapport with the interviewer.

The following is a general outline of various types of interviews that are commonly used by human resources professionals, hiring managers and recruiters.

Connecting the Resumé to the Interview Process

In the resumé chapter of this book, you were asked to write your accomplishments down in a sentence that included the result of what you had achieved. By doing an exercise like this, and subsequently creating your resumé, you were in fact preparing your stories for the interview process. When writing these stories, you are giving the reader a taste of what you can potentially do in the future, so that during the interview you will be able to fill in the details of the story.

Each accomplishment you have written about includes a component of your ability to solve various problems. Here are some examples and what they show the interviewer.

✧ **Developed continuous process improvements within billing production, resulting in invoices being delivered to customers in an accurate and timely fashion.**

The above demonstrates the ability to develop a new process that increases accuracy and saves time.

✧ **Initiated an employee opinion survey that resulted in the implementation of new policies and procedures and significantly increased morale.**

The above demonstrates the ability to use a creative approach to resolve moral issues with employees, and the ability to take action to implement new procedures.

Exercise

- You now need to go back to your resumé and review it carefully. Look at the different skills and abilities that each accomplishment is able to demonstrate to an employer. This information can also be used during an evaluation.
- You can take this one step further by reviewing the behavioral questions in this chapter and matching the competencies that are listed i.e.: *adaptability, efficiency, team work, analytical thinking, etc.* The process is the same as above: match each of your accomplishments with the competencies required for the job.

What are Competencies?

The definition of a competency is any skill, knowledge, behavior or other personal characteristic that is essential to perform the job, or differentiates the average performers from those who perform at a superior level.

By following the exercise above, you will be prepared for any questions that are asked during an interview. Another tip is to create an additional list of accomplishments that are not shown on the resumé.

Types of Interviews

Emotional intelligence interview

➤ This interview style is used to determine how you manage both your relationships and yourself. It focuses on such areas as self-awareness, self-regulation, motivation, empathy and social awareness.

Situational interview

➤ The interviewer will describe a specific situation and ask you to discuss how you would handle the situation or ask you to describe how you have handled the situation in the past.

Informational interview

➤ The purpose of the informational interview is to gather information about the company and/or industry for future opportunities. This is a great opportunity for a candidate to learn, discover hidden jobs and get referrals.

Panel interview

➤ The purpose of a panel interview is to allow more than one person at a time to meet with the prospective candidate. It gives the interviewers an opportunity to compare notes immediately after the interview is completed.

Succession interview

➤ The purpose of a succession interview is to allow the management team and peers on the team to meet a prospective candidate individually and in one day.

Stress interview

➤ The purpose of a stress interview is to observe how well a candidate manages under stress. This type of interview is often used on management and senior customer service representatives.

Presentation interview

➤ The purpose of the presentation interview is to observe a candidate's ability to make a presentation in front of clients and management. This type of interview is often given to sales and management candidates.

Behavioral interview

➤ Individuals who use the behavioral interviewing style believe in the theory that *past performance is the best predictor of future performance.*

➤ The interviewer will ask such questions as, *"Tell me about a time when you...."*

➤ This interviewing style is all about you and your stories.

How the Behavioral Interview Works

It is important to take a closer look at behavioral interviews and gain a deeper understanding of the reasons behind since this is the format of most interviews in today's job market.

Research and experience has proven that
- across all job categories, some people perform much more effectively than others;
- superior performers use different approaches and behaviors; and
- past performance is the best predictor of future performance.

Behavioral interviewing:
- builds rapport;
- sticks to issues related to the job; and
- ensures the interviewer gets the information by extensive probing of a candidate's story.

Behavioral interviewing does not influence the candidate with personal reactions from the interviewer. If interviewers are trained in this technique, their goal is to focus and listen to the answers of the candidate and not to give their opinion about the story.

Behavioral interviewing prevents the following from happening:

- **Halo Effect**—This happens when a potential applicant is referred by someone else (i.e. a best friend, the manager of the department you work for, VP's brother, etc.) and the interviewer is told the person is amazing. There is already a preconceived idea that the potential candidate will be a good fit.

- **Order Effect**—This can happen when an organization has an order to fill and they are desperate. The potential candidate has all the hard skills and past experience at another company in the same industry so the interviewer may overlook details about the candidate's personality and ability to actually get the job done.

- **Similar-to-Me Effect**—This is among the biggest mistakes made by hiring managers. Don't we just love people who are just like us? If an interviewer falls into this trap, however, they again risk overlooking important information about the candidate's ability to do the job and fit into the corporation.

- **Stereotypes**—This includes disqualification of candidates because they are too young, too old, a man is needed, or people from the telecommunications industry do not fit into our environment, etc.

The behavioral interview levels the playing field for everyone because it speaks to what the person has actually accomplished, not just who they are.

C.A.R. and How It Will Assist You during the Interview Process

Many of us become nervous during an interview and can go off on a tangent when answering a question. This can result in losing the interviewer and the opportunity to demonstrate what it is you can do for the potential employer. There is nothing worse for an interviewer than an applicant rambling on and not giving the correct answer to the question asked. Your goal is to capture and engage the attention of the interviewer so that person remembers you. This can be easily done if you apply the C.A.R. technique we discussed earlier in the book

When you are asked a behavioral question, answer what the *challenge* was, the *actions* that you took to resolve the challenge, and then end with the *result*. If you end with the result, that will be the last thing left in the interviewer's mind. The interviewer will retain the impression that you are a person who can get things done.

Here are some examples of questions and answers that can help you prepare for a job interview.

Question: Give me an example of a time when you had to cut costs in your department and how you were able to do that.
Answer: The challenge was to cut costs while maintaining the head count we currently had because our workload was expected to increase over the next quarter.

I decided that instead of just crunching numbers I would take a creative approach and give the team an opportunity to help me solve the problem. So, I invited them to a meeting along with a senior finance person and we reviewed our expenses. We discovered that we were overspending on outside consultants for work that could be done in-house. We also discovered that everyone was using same-day couriers for everything that was being delivered. I then created and implemented a process that would determine if work that was to be given to an outside consultant could in fact be done in-house. Next, we developed and implemented a new process for determining if same-day shipment expenses were necessary, or if these deliveries could be included with the biweekly shipments.

The result was that we immediately started to save $10,000 per month in consulting and shipment costs. It also meant that the team was getting the opportunity to develop new skills and work on projects that were normally only assigned to outside consultants.

The idea to answering in this format is that it gives you the opportunity to stay on track, be concise and stick to the questions. Not every question has a numbers-qualified answer. You need, therefore, to look at the outcome or result from a different point of view. The example above has two outcomes—the dollar value and the fact that the employees had the opportunity to develop skills and work on projects that would normally be sent to a consultant. Other examples of outcomes/results might include: information is easier to access, there is a more cohesive team environment, you saved one hour per day, saved the client from giving the business to another vendor, etc.

If you are still uncertain, review the resumé chapter and resumé samples for ideas on how to demonstrate results.

Behavioral Interviewing Questions

When answering the following questions, apply the **C.A.R.** method. This stops you from going off on a tangent and keeps you on track when you are answering a question during an interview. It also gives you a clear and direct way of answering a question so that the interviewer can have a complete understanding of the challenge you faced, the actions you took to resolve the challenge, and the end result. Check your resumé for answers to some of the questions below.

1. Listening, Understanding and Responding

This is the ability to accurately listen and understand, and then respond appropriately when interacting with individuals and groups. Examples of questions are:

➤ Tell me of a time in your work experience when a customer requested your input/ advice on an emotionally charged issue. What steps did you take to ensure understanding of the problem before offering an opinion?

➤ Tell me of a time in your work experience when you were required to provide counsel to an emotionally distraught colleague/subordinate. What interpersonal skills did you use to gain a better understanding of the individual's problem?

➤ Tell me of a time in your work experience when you were able to get at the root cause of an individual's or group's emotional behavior. What techniques did you use?

➤ Tell me about a time when you were required to deal with a conflict or resolve a dispute.

➤ Describe a time when you had to understand another person's point of view in order to solve a problem.

2. Achievement Motivation (Results Orientation)

This is a concern for working well or for surpassing a standard of excellence. The standard may be one's own past performance (striving for improvement), an objective measure, outperforming others (competitiveness), challenging goals one has set or even that which has never been accomplished before (innovation). Examples of questions are:

➤ Of the jobs you have held, which one represents your very best work? What was it about this job that enabled or motivated you to do your best work?

➤ Tell me about a time in your work experience when tracking your personal performance against established goals enhanced your ability to meet those goals?

➤ Tell me about a time in your work experience when you initiated a change (e.g. in work methods, in operating procedures) in order to improve your work performance.

➤ Tell me about a time when you were tasked with very aggressive performance goals. What steps did you take to optimize your chances of achieving them? Were you successful?

➤ Tell me about a time in your work experience when you acted purely on instinct (i.e. without analysis or precedent) to pursue an exciting business opportunity. What was the result? Would you adopt this approach again?

➤ Tell me about a time in your work experience when you analyzed the effectiveness of your business to determine whether the structure and processes were hindering results. What was the outcome? What changes did you implement? How did this affect organizational performance?

➤ Typically, what type of analysis have you used to measure the team's performance relative to its goals? In the case where goals have not been met, what corrective action have you taken?

➤ Tell me about a recent accomplishment.

➤ Can you give me an example of a work-related goal you met and what was the outcome?

3. Efficiency

This is the ability to complete transactions efficiently and in full compliance with procedures. It is also the ability to find ways to accomplish the most with limited time and resources. Examples of questions are:

➤ Tell me about a time when you had to work to a deadline.

➤ Tell me about a time when you had multiple tasks to perform. What did you do?

4. Teamwork

This is the ability to work co-operatively within the team/work group and across the organization to achieve group and organizational goals.

➢ Describe a situation where you had difficulty getting co-operation from team members and how you handled it.

➢ Tell me about a time when you felt particularly effective as a member of a team.

5. Adaptability

This is the ability to adapt to and work effectively within a variety of situations, and with various individuals or groups. Adaptability entails understanding and appreciating different and opposing perspectives on an issue, adapting one's approach as the requirements of a situation change, and changing or easily accepting changes in one's job, organization or customer/partner organizations. Examples of questions are:

➢ Tell me about a time when an event you had planned for did not materialize for some reason and what you did.

➢ Tell me about a time when you had to change your point of view or your plans to take into account new information or another person's preference.

➢ Tell me of a time when you held a strong, passionate view about a business issue, idea or strategy, and found that your peers held divergent views from yours. What did you do?

➢ We often get used to a particular way of doing things. Give me an example of a time when a colleague or employer implemented an alternative approach and describe your response to it.

➢ While it is important to respect rules and procedures, sometimes they can block actions necessary to the achievement of a goal or to resolving a problem. Describe a time in your work experience when this happened to you. What did you do?

➢ Sometimes it is necessary to change the way we do things in order to implement a new idea or project successfully. Give me an example of a time when you veered from your traditional approach to ensure that your desired goal or outcome was reached. How did you feel? In retrospect, is there anything you would have done differently?

➤ Describe a time in your work experience when you recognized the need to completely abandon/overhaul a long-term strategy and "start over, from scratch." What prompted you to act (e.g. changed circumstance, new information)? Who was affected by your decision? What was the outcome?

6. Analytical Thinking

The analytical thinking interview is used to test your understanding of a situation by breaking it apart into smaller pieces, or tracing the implications of a situation in a step-by-step way. Analytical thinking includes organizing the parts of a problem, situation, etc. in a systematic way, making systematic comparisons of different features or aspects, setting priorities on a rational basis, identifying time sequences, causal relationships or 'if-then' relationships. Examples of questions are:

➤ Describe the approach you take to solve a problem.

➤ Describe the process you use to analyze a problem and to develop solutions.

➤ Problems that we anticipate are generally easier to solve than those that take us by surprise. Describe a time in your work experience when you carefully analyzed a project plan for potential problems. How did this 'proactive' approach help you to prevent those problems from occurring?

➤ Describe a work-related problem or situation for which you developed several alternative solutions. How did you go about developing each solution? How did you go about selecting the most appropriate course of action? What was the outcome? Given a second chance, would you still have chosen that course of action?

➤ Describe a time in your work experience when you were faced with a multi-dimensional problem that affected several interest groups. What approach did you take to resolving the problem? What role did each interest group take?

➤ Describe a time in your work experience when you were responsible for resolving a pervasive and complex problem that spanned many organizational functions. How did you develop a solution or solutions that would satisfy many interdependent systems?

➤ Describe a complex job-related problem you encountered and how you solved it.

7. Impact and Influence

This interview style demonstrates how to persuade, convince, influence or impress others in order to motivate them to act alone or to support one's purpose. It is based on having the desire to have a specific positive impact or effect on others where the person has a specific type of impression to make or a course of action that s/he wants the other(s) to adopt. Examples of questions are:

➤ Describe a time in your work experience where the need for action or change was evident to you but would be unpopular with others. How did you first introduce the need?

➤ Describe a time in your work experience when you recognized that you would have to persuade someone (e.g. a customer, staff member, manager) to adopt a specific course of action. What steps did you take? Were you successful?

➤ It's often been said that timing is everything. Recount a work experience where, by all indications, the timing was 'finally right' to push for your idea. Describe the optimal conditions that were present and the persuasive action that you took.

➤ Describe a time when you were charged with influencing the opinions of a diverse group (e.g. varied interests, motives, outcomes). What methods did you use to ensure that they would be persuaded to share your view?

➤ Recount a time in your work experience when you chose a highly unorthodox approach (e.g. creative, dramatic, unusual) to persuade a group. What made you choose this approach? What factors did you consider?

➤ Describe a time when you relied on others to influence or persuade on your behalf since their actions would best further your goal.

➤ Tell me about a time when it was important to effect attitudinal change on a large scale. Describe the strategy that you developed and implemented to promote influence and persuade change.

➤ Describe a recent situation in which you convinced an individual or a group to do something.

➤ Tell me about a situation when you got others to adopt your ideas.

8. Business Acumen

This interview tests your ability to identify business opportunities and to implement successful business strategies. It requires an awareness of business issues, processes and outcomes as they impact both the organization's and customer's strategic direction. Examples of questions are:

➤ In what ways does your current/most recent role impact the company's profitability? Ideally, how would you change your role to be better aligned with the company's bottom line?

➤ Tell me about the most pressing business issue facing your group currently or over the next ___ months. Why is it important/problematic? What are you doing about it? How might it affect the broader organization?

➤ On a quarterly basis, it's important for managers to analyze their business unit's productivity. What business variables have you analyzed? What were the findings? How well do they support the company's strategic priorities? What changes have you made to ensure optimal alignment with the company's strategic priorities?

➤ Describe the steps that you have taken historically to ensure that your business unit's goals are in alignment with the company's goals.

➤ Describe how you go about balancing the challenge of revenue growth and cost control when making decisions that impact the business.

➤ Describe a time from your recent work experience when you were able to use constructive feedback offered by a client/partner/peer to improve your business unit's profitability.

➤ Tell me of a time in your work experience when your efforts to add value to a client positively impacted your business unit. What behaviors and/or actions did you display? How can these behaviors and/or actions be adapted to other client relationships?

➤ Describe a time in your recent work experience when you were able to recombine your company's products/services to expand your client base. What conditions/information/realization led you to this idea?

➤ Describe a time in your work experience when you envisioned a new product/service (or a new application for an existing product/service) and felt compelled to bring it to market. Outline the steps you took as well as the hurdles you overcame to advance your vision. What was the outcome?

➤ Describe a time in your work experience when a staff reorganization resulted in improved synergy and renewed creative energy. What new business opportunities or competitive advantage emerged?

➤ Tell me about a time when you were able to create an advantage for your company based on your knowledge of a key competitor's strategic activities. What counter- strategies did you put into place for your group?

➤ Describe your most recent work experience in which you held complete responsibility for the company's strategic direction.

➤ What inputs (resources, information) were key to guiding your formulation of strategies for the organization as a whole.

➤ How did you go about setting standards of excellence for every facet of the organization?

➤ How have you optimized the quality and scope of your service mandate within the international community?

9. Change Leadership

This interview is designed to understand an applicant's ability to effectively communicate the change agenda and gain commitment to the changed vision. Examples of questions are:

➤ Tell me about a time when you identified a need for organizational change. Describe the thoughts and considerations that led you to this conclusion. How did you go about communicating the need for change initially?

➤ Describe a time in your experience as a 'change leader' when you had to communicate the need for change to stakeholders.

➤ In promoting the need for change, describe your 'vision' and how you went about communicating it and the benefits that would result. What steps did you take to sell the change?

➤ It's sometimes said that people only hear what they want to hear. What measures did you put into place within your organization to ensure that the change initiative was well-communicated and reinforced regularly?

➤ Humans are largely creatures of habit, preferring 'the way we've always done it' to change. Tell me of a time in your experience as a change leader when you were able to build support for change by publicly challenging the 'tried and true' conventions of the company.

➤ Describe a time in your experience as a change leader when you progressed beyond 'change communications' to taking a visible step toward implementation. What was that step? How was it received? How did you mediate the reaction?

➤ In your efforts to 'create a new future" for your company, describe for me, from inception to completion, the largest-scale organizational change that you have championed. What cultural goals did you have in mind when you conceived of the change? What strategic goals did you have in mind when you conceived of the change? Were these met? What key behaviors did you demonstrate and model to promote acceptance for change?

10. Customer Focus

This interview style implies a desire to help or serve customers, to meet their needs. It means focusing one's efforts on discovering and meeting the customer's needs, while balancing those needs against our business and strategic priorities. Customers may be broadly defined, including final customers, distributors, or internal customers or clients. Examples of questions are:

➤ Tell me about a time when you had to deal with a customer who expressed dissatisfaction with you or your company and how you dealt with it?

➤ Describe a time when a client/user asked you for something that was especially difficult to do or provide?

➤ Tell me about a time in your work experience when customer service was the most important aspect of the job. What work behaviors were essential to providing optimal customer service in that job?

➤ Tell me about a time in your work experience when you neglected to follow up on a specific client request. What was the outcome? What did you learn?

➤ Tell me about a time when circumstances beyond your control led to a customer service problem. How did you handle this situation?

➤ Tell me about a time when you were faced with a customer service problem but conventional approaches were not enough to resolve the issue. What did you do?

➤ What is the most positive compliment you have received from a customer? What was the circumstance that prompted it?

➤ Typically, how do you go about collecting information about your customer's business?

➤ Tell me your approach to discovering the underlying needs of your most important customer.

➤ Tell me about a time when your opinion of what the customer needed was in conflict with the expressed need. What did you do?

➤ What measures have you taken in past work experiences to ensure a long-term relationship with the customer?

11. Integrity and Honesty

This interview is used to determine whether a candidate's actions are consistent with one's personal values and beliefs, as well as the company's professional and business ethics. S/he 'walks the talk', communicates intentions, ideas and feelings openly and directly, in a sensitive and tactful manner. Examples of questions are:

➤ Tell me about a time in your work experience when you revealed the truth about a situation that was important to the company but would implicate a co-worker.

➤ Tell me about a time when you had to terminate your 'star performer' due to suspicious behavior or unethical business practices.

➤ Describe a time in your work experience when you knew that your company's business proposal had serious drawbacks or weaknesses that might lead to unanticipated costs for the client.

Traditional Style Interviewing Questions

What do you know about our organization?

If you have done your homework, you can honestly say that you have studied all that is publicly available about the organization and are thus aware of many published facts. However, you might also state that you would like to know more. In that case, you should be prepared to ask intelligent questions.

What important trends do you see coming in our industry?

Choose two or three important developments to discuss. This is an opportunity to show that you have thought about the future, the economics, the markets, the technology of the industry, and that you have done your research.

In your last position, what were the things that you liked most? Liked least?

Respond with care to this question. Create a list of must have, flexibilities and dislikes. You will want to emphasize the positives and de-emphasize the negatives.

What motivates you the most?

Answers may include the satisfaction of meeting the challenges of the position, developing teams and individuals, meeting organizational goals.

What are your long-range goals?

Relate your answer to the company you are interviewing with rather than giving a very broad, general answer. Keep your ambitions realistic. First, talk about doing the work for which you are applying, then talk about longer-range goals.

Tell me about yourself.

This is your introduction (nearly every interviewer asks this question), and here you are building rapport and giving the interviewer a frame of reference. Talk past, present, and what you hope to do in the future. Think of your profile when organizing this answer.

Why are you seeking a position with our company?

Indicate that from your study of the company, the business issues they face are the kind that excite you and match up well with your skills, abilities and past experience. If you can do so honestly, express your admiration for the company and what it is that appeals to you.

How would you describe your personality?

Mention two or three of your most beneficial traits. To the extent that you can, highlight traits that would be a valuable asset to the work challenge under discussion.

What is your management style?

You might want to talk about how you set goals and then get your people involved in them. Also, describe the techniques that you like to use to bring out the best in people, using the most appropriate style to fit the situation.

Your research may have given you a sense of whether the company believes in a highly participative style or is more authoritarian in its approach. If you don't know the company's style, keep your answer situational and refer to examples from your accomplishments.

Why are you leaving your present job?

This question must be answered briefly. If you get defensive or explain and rationalize to excess, you will only stir up questions and concerns in the interviewer's mind. If it was a forced reduction due to economic circumstances, make that clear.

If possible, explain how your termination was not a single lay-off but part of a large group reduction. When you have finished answering, look the interviewer in the eye and stop talking.

What do you feel would be an ideal work environment?

This is an opportunity to give insights about what satisfies you, but remember to stay grounded.

Looking back, how do you perceive your past employer?

Be positive. Refer to the valuable experience you have gained. Never bad-mouth a former employer, no matter how justified. Say something neutral, "It is an excellent company which has given me many valuable experiences and opportunities to perform successfully."

How do you think your subordinates perceive you?

Be as positive as you can, referring to your strengths, skills and traits, but remember to be honest, too. References are easily checked.

Why haven't you found a new position after so many months?

You may find this question offensive, but try not to take it personally. Simply give a brief answer such as, "Finding any position in this marketplace is challenging, but finding the right position takes care and time," and then move on.

What do you think of your previous manager?

Be as positive as you can, and avoid becoming embroiled in this issue. If you like the individual, say so and tell why. If you don't, think of something positive to say.

What sort of relationships do you have with your business partners, at the same level and above and below you?

This is an important question, so you will want to take the time to answer it in logical steps. When talking about your relationships with subordinates, be prepared to state your management philosophy, particularly with regard to performance issues.

When speaking of managers, indicate your keen interest in understanding your manager's expectations, so that you and your organization can build your goals in a way that will support his or her goals. You may also want to talk about how you would keep your manager informed. Stress your team-building and mutually co-operative approach with peers.

What can you offer us that other candidates cannot?

Respond by emphasizing your unique qualities and capabilities. Relate them to the position at hand whenever possible.

What are your strengths?

You should be able to enumerate three or four of your key strengths (with examples) that are relevant to their needs based on your research and other data you have gathered about the company.

How successful have you been so far?

Be prepared to define success for yourself and then respond. Try to choose accomplishments that relate to the organization's needs and values if you have been able to determine that from your research.

What are your limitations? Tell me about a time when your work was criticized. What was your biggest business mistake?

Responding with a strength that, if overdone, could be considered a weakness can be a problem. Professionals in most organizations are familiar with this technique and may consider it to be evasive. When discussing mistakes or criticism, emphasize what you learned and how your behavior is different as a result of the experience. Do not claim to be faultless.

What qualifications do you have that you feel would make you successful here?

If the question is asked early on, talk about two or three of your major skills and, to the extent that you can, relate them to the company. If this question is asked after you have sufficient information about the position, talk about two or three of your major problem-solving skills (supported by accomplishments) that you believe will be useful in the position.

How long would it take you to make a meaningful contribution to our firm?

More and more companies are looking for people who can 'hit the ground running.' They don't have time to bring people up to speed with on-the-job training. Again, the timing of the question is important. Do you know enough about the specific position to give a cogent response? Ask the interviewer his/her expectations.

Can you describe how you solved a difficult management problem?

Relate one of your accomplishments that had to do with this kind of situation. Depending on the organization's culture and needs, highlight conflict management, team building or staffing.

As a manager, have you ever had to fire anyone? If so, what were the circumstances and how did you handle it?

If you have, answer briefly that you have indeed had this experience and that it worked out to the benefit of both the individual and the organization. You followed the company's disciplinary procedures carefully before proceeding to termination. (The company may be concerned about discrimination and legal issues.) Don't volunteer more information unless the interviewer asks for more details.

If you have never fired anyone, say so, but talk about how you would utilize progressive discipline before resorting to termination to protect the company's best interests.

What do you see as the most difficult task in being a manager?

Your answer might address your ability to delegate, getting things planned and completed on time within the budget, maintaining high standards, or other management issues.

What were some situations in which you worked under pressure or met deadlines?

Refer to your accomplishments. Discuss one or two in which you were especially effective in meeting deadlines or dealing with high-pressure situations. Be the knight in shinning armour.

Can you tell me about an objective in your last job that you failed to meet? Why?

Discuss an objective which you renegotiated when you realized it could not be met because of obstacles beyond your control.

Above all, state what you learned as a result of the experience.

What have you done that helped increase sales or profit? How did you go about it?

This is a great chance to describe in some detail a business accomplishment that is relevant to the proposed new position.

How much financial responsibility have you had in previous positions?

You can answer this in terms of your budget, head count, or the size of the project or sales team that you directed.

How many people have you managed in your recent positions?

Give examples of times when you were a leader. Draw examples from accomplishments that demonstrate your leadership skills. Remember to keep all descriptions brief.

In your most recent position, what were some of your most significant accomplishments?

Since you have already selected the specific accomplishments you want to talk about, this question will be simple to answer. Be ready to describe three or four of them. When possible, try to relate your answer to the nature of the new challenges you might be facing.

If I spoke with your previous manager, what would he or she say are your greatest strengths and weaknesses?

Be consistent with what you think he or she would say. Talk about any weakness in a positive way. Use examples, not just words. Your former manager will probably want to give you a good reference, so recount some of the positive things you did for him or her.

Give one or two examples of your creativity. Refer to accomplishments that relate to the company and the position, if possible.

Don't Get Hung up on the Words!

Remember that the interviewing process is not just about what you say. The interviewer is also observing your body language, the tone of your voice, facial expressions, how you dress and so much more. After all, 55% of all communication is body language with tone at 38% and the actual words amount to only 7% of all language!

What Questions to Ask during the Interview

The biggest mistake you can make in an interview is to spend the whole interview anticipating the interviewer's questions and how you are going to answer. The other mistake is to go to an interview with the 'pick me—I will and can do anything' attitude. When you are not present in an interview and spend your time anticipating and molding and twisting yourself into the perfect candidate, you may succeed in securing a position that is not suited to you. Remember the ISO story in the resumé chapter!

The interview process is not just about the company and its needs. It is also about you and your needs. You need to be fully present during the interview so that you are aware of what is happening around you—from the person interviewing you, to the environment, to the atmosphere—so that you can make a fully informed decision about the opportunity and the company.

Josie secured an interview with her dream company. She had specifically targeted the company and had networked her way into an interview with the president of the company. She arrived five minutes early and walked up to the receptionist's desk and waited as the receptionist answered the phone. Not once during the time that Josie stood there did the receptionist's head rise to acknowledge Josie's presence. Finally, the receptionist looked up. Josie gave her name and whom she was there to see. The receptionist abruptly told her to have a seat.

It was the end of the day and as Josie sat in the receptionist's area she noticed that there was a lot of activity with people rushing back and forth. One man even passed her three times in a period of 20 minutes. Not once during that time did the receptionist speak to Josie or explain why the president of the company had not appeared. "I also noticed that not one person looked directly at me or smiled. There was no warmth. Everyone was rushing back and forth without a word to say to each other."

Josie approached the receptionist and asked her if the president would be much longer. The receptionist explained that he was finishing up a few things and would be with her shortly. Fifteen minutes later he appeared and introduced himself. He was the guy that had passed Josie on three occasions without a word while she sat in the lobby.

The president of the company brought Josie into a boardroom without even a comment on the fact the he had left her waiting for approximately 45 minutes. He then proceeded to question her on her resumé. Just as Josie started to feel comfortable and the conversation began to flow, someone walked by the open boardroom door. The president called him into the room and asked him a series of questions about a project that he was obviously working on. After the employee left, the president turned to Josie and asked, "Where were we?"

Josie was shocked. "He was so easily distracted, the conversation had no focus. He never closed the door and looked at the door every few minutes to see what was going on in the hall. I wanted to ask if I should come back another time when things were not so chaotic. I suspected, however, that that was his personality and the environment he had created."

Josie had prepared a series of questions and most were not answered. Continually, the president would go off on tangents about himself. "When I asked him what he would expect the person he hired to accomplish in the first six months into the position, he said he had not given it any thought. I then asked him what the ideal skills and competencies were that he wanted for the person in this position. He just laughed and said, 'It depends.' He did not answer one question directly. I could not imagine working for this person or working in such a crazy environment. I don't believe that you can be successful if you do not have set goals and you cannot get a straight answer from the person with the power."

Josie was surprised when the human resources person called her three days later to ask her to come back to the company and meet the team. "I immediately declined. My gut instinct went into overdrive and was screaming, 'NO' from the time I stepped foot in the receptionist's area."

Josie was present during the interview process from the minute she walked into the building. She noticed the atmosphere, the way people treated each other and the way she was treated. Finally, she was painfully aware of how her questions were being answered by the individual whom she would report to. Have you ever been hired for a position that later turned out to be a disaster and, when you think back to the interviewing process, the signs were all there?

Your questions need to be developed from what it is that is most important to you. Josie wanted clear direction, set goals and an executive team that had a vision for the future. She was able to create questions around her individual preferences.

The best thing to do is to write down your key *I Wants*. For example:

1. I want clear communication and expectations.

2. I want training. It is very important to me to make sure I am always marketable.

3. I am looking for a specific leadership or management style.

4. I am looking for an opportunity for promotion.

Your questions may look like this:

5. What are the expectations and goals for the first six months?

6. What type of training can I expect to have access to over the course of a year? Do you have specific in-house training, or do you rely on outside training? What are some of the training programs offered to an employee? Is there an allotted amount of money spent or given to an employee on a yearly basis?

7. Could you give me an example of your leadership style when dealing with employees in a challenging situation i.e., a deadline not met?

8. Do you have a formal succession plan in place? Have you promoted anyone in the last year in your department? How do you determine when an employee is ready to move into the next position?

The examples above give a very basic overview of how to match questions with your needs and wants. You need to take the time to sit down and determine what it is you need and want and then develop the questions. You can also go to the company's web site before developing your questions. For instance, if you noticed on the web site that they have just acquired a new company, you may want to ask the hiring manager how that acquisition has affected his or her department, or what the effect has been on the company in general. These are informed questions that will help you appear knowledgeable, without being a know-it-all.

It is very important to state what you know with a question that solicits an opinion just in case the person you are being interviewed by is not up-to-date on what is going on. If you position the information you have gained this way, you will be able to ascertain the interviewer's knowledge without making them look foolish or less informed than you.

Flexible Thinker Tool #4
Relax

Take a deep breath and say to yourself,

"1, 2, 3—Relax!"

When you relax you allow yourself to be in the moment and seize the opportunities that are presented to you. You also allow yourself to connect with your body.

Have you ever been in a tense situation where all you could do was stand there and stammer? Later, you go home and while you are lying in bed thinking about the situation you say to yourself, "Geez, I should have said that! That would have really turned the situation around!" The reason that you could think of something to say that night but could not think of it earlier, is that you are now relaxed. It is easy to relax when you are getting that hot oil massage and the rain forest music is playing in the background. The trick is to learn to relax when you are in a pressure situation.

As I was driving my car, I tuned into a radio station talk show where they were interviewing a professor from the University of California at Berkeley. He was discussing his latest research on the common characteristics of the most successful CEOs in America. He had found only two common characteristics. The first was that the executives all had very diverse backgrounds. For instance, Jack Welsh, the former CEO of General Electric, started off with a degree in chemical engineering, next worked as a consultant, and then had different jobs within GE before becoming the CEO.

The other thing that all of the executives had in common was that when they were faced with a difficult decision, one that could dramatically affect their company, they took a moment and went somewhere quiet where they could get in touch with their 'gut instinct.' They then made the decision based on what that was saying to them.

The part that I found most interesting was what the professor hypothesized about the subconscious. He used the metaphor of a computer to explain that your conscious mind, which makes up about 8 percent of your brain functioning, is like the RAM in a computer and that the other 92 percent of your brain is like the hard drive. Everything you have seen, heard, and experienced in your entire lifetime goes into that hard drive that you call your subconscious mind. Then, when you are faced with a situation, the data is put into the hard drive and your brain processes all of the information and looks for a common trend. Since there is so much data—the information collected over a lifetime of experiences and knowledge—your subconscious brain cannot possibly relay all that information to your conscious mind, so it communicates to it via the 'gut instinct'—when you just know something to be true, but you do not know why. So, far from being an illogical decision, the gut instinct is based on the most logical—the common trend of your entire life experiences.

What Is the Gut Instinct?

- Comes into play when we are faced with several options but for some reason we get a strong 'feeling' that a certain one is the way to go.
- Actually a logical decision based on trends gathered from all the experiences stored in your subconscious.
- The subconscious mind's way of communicating with the conscious mind.
- A function of the subconscious, the gut instinct is a crucial part of being able to make choices under pressure.

Your fourth tool—**RELAX**
Relax means to *Relax!*

Ways to Relax under Pressure

We all have fear which causes stress. As we said earlier, it is at this time that we need to *relax* the most! Look at the world of sports. What separates the winners from the losers in a competitive situation? Why is it that, even though the competitors (especially at an elite level) are almost identical physically and in terms of skill level, there are people who excel and succeed while others freeze and fail? The winners have developed the ability to use fear to their advantage. They *orange* fear as an opportunity. Jack Nicklaus, the legendary golfer, provides an example of this attitude. He once commented that he actually finds the big tournaments the easier ones to win. "In (the major tournaments) you knew that, when it got closer to the final day, the pack ahead of you would fall back because of the pressure," Nicklaus said.

How to Stay Relaxed under Pressure

- **Imagine the best.** Think positively! See yourself doing well in the interview and showing what you can do.
- **Put the situation in perspective.** There are always more opportunities.
- **Practice under pressure.** Repetition decreases fear. Do mock interviews with a friend or recruiter.
- **Be prepared.** Do your homework on the industry, company, etc. The better prepared you are, the easier it will be to concentrate on what is happening in the interview and be 'in the now.'
- **Focus on your motivation.** Why is this opportunity right for you and what can you bring to the table?

We have all had moments where we have had that gut instinct, ignored it, and later regretted it. There is always tension in any interview situation. You have a lot at stake and there is competition. Remember this—you know all of the answers. You know if this is the right opportunity for you. The answer is in your gut.

The key to being able to access it, however, is to **relax**. Be in the moment, see all that is around you, hear what is being said and then feel with your gut to decide if it is right for you.

This is a crucial tool to use during an interview. As we mentioned earlier in this chapter, it is vital during an interview to be in the present. Remembering the 'Relax' keyword will allow you to be in the moment so that you can keep in touch with your gut instinct.

Chapter Seven:

Negotiating for Me Inc.

Am I not destroying my enemies
when I make friends of them?
ABRAHAM LINCOLN

Jerry, who sells real estate, says everything is negotiable. "I have to negotiate every day," he says. 'Even when I go to the mall, I negotiate the price that is listed. I love negotiating. To me it is fun."

I have been to the mall with Jerry, and sometimes his attitude can be annoying. "Why don't you just accept the price listed?" I ask him.

"Because I enjoy the game," he replies. "Besides, it keeps my skills sharp. I have never understood why people would want lawyers to negotiate for them. Most of them are mediocre negotiators to say the least. The person whom you want to represent for you is a person whose entire income is dependent on their negotiating skills. Give me a real estate agent, car salesperson, or headhunter any day. They know how to ask the right questions and get the best results."

Jerry has a point. You never know until you ask. Yet, for a number of reasons we are often afraid to do so. We worry that if we ask for too much, we may not get the position we want. Although it is true that everything is negotiable, there are a number of factors to consider when you are negotiating a job offer.

Sara did not need the car allowance or the car that her company offered her. After all, her father had already bought and paid for a brand new car when her first child was born. Instead, she wanted the money to be applied to daycare expenses. The human resources manager was at first skeptical and told Sara that she had never seen a car allowance applied to daycare. Sara did not see this as a problem. She felt it was worth the effort to try and negotiate this into her contract for the position she was being offered.

After a series of discussions with the human resources manager, the hiring manager and other senior executives, Sara was given the car allowance money for daycare. She was thrilled. "All they can do is say no. If it is a yes, however, you can't help but feel how powerful just asking can be," Sara said jubilantly.

This is the final stage of the career management process. You have put together your resumé, found the position and gone through the interview. The company or organization is now interested enough in you to discuss terms of employment. How well you negotiate may not only have a direct influence on what you receive from your potential employer in terms of salary, benefits, etc., but it could also have a significant impact on the amount of respect that you receive within the company. It may even have an effect on whether you get the job or not. Let's 'orange' this for one minute. You are not negotiating for yourself or even for '*Me Inc.*', you are demonstrating to your potential employer how sharp your negotiation skills are. Remember that after you get the job, you may well be called upon to negotiate on behalf of the company and they will want somebody who can represent them effectively.

Win-Win

There have been many books and articles written about win-win negotiations. For employment, this is the only way to truly negotiate for a job. If you lose or the company loses, a win-lose outcome will quickly poison the atmosphere.

What is win-win? It really means understanding both your own needs and those of your potential employer. If you cannot achieve win-win, your best option may be to walk away or look at this as a short-term fix and immediately start looking for other career alternatives.

Here are the steps to a win-win negotiation:

- **Research and prepare yourself in advance.** The more you understand about the company, their 'I Wants', their demands, the better you can negotiate with them to achieve your goal.

- **Listen carefully and assertively to what is being said by the other side.** Have alternatives ready.

- **Build on the ideas presented by the other side.** The more alternatives you can create, the more likely you will be to have a successful negotiation.

- **Don't be afraid to ask.** If you don't understand the whats and whys, ask so that you do.

- **Relax.** Enjoy the process and learn from it. You have to be able to relax under pressure in order to really understand what is happening.

Preparing for the Negotiation— Navigate and Negotiate

What are the factors that were discussed in assessing the best idea? This is a yardstick that you can apply to all of the ideas created and how they apply to the job market. Here are the four factors you need to examine before you start negotiating.

- **Assess the culture.** Does the company have a large turnover and if so, why? What is the culture of the area you are going to be working in like?

- **Understand external factors.** What are your critical needs and what are your secondary needs? What shape is the industry in generally and the company in specifically? What are their constraints in giving you what you need?

- **Explore strengths.** What are the strengths that you are bringing to the position? Will your strengths be sufficiently utilized and does the position work to those strengths?

- **Look at the environment.** What is the current market like for your skills? Has the position been open for a long time? Have others refused it? Are your skills rare in the market-place, or can they be readily found in someone else?

In spite of what Jerry said, not everything is necessarily nego-tiable. He is right when he claims that you don't know until you ask. For instance, money left on the negotiating table is lost forev-er. In an employment situation, that loss accumulates exponentially when you consider that bonus and merit increases are often based on your base compensation.

The Flexible Negotiator

Demonstrate flexibility in your negotiations. We will introduce other *Flexible Thinker*® tools to help you during this period. Here are some ways that you can use the tools we have already discussed:

- **Don't take it personally.** Remember, you are negotiating for your company, *Me Inc.*, and not you as an individual.

- **Orange** it as *Game*. It can be something fun and challenging instead of dreadful.

- **Orange** it as *Opportunity*. By showing how well you can negotiate for *Me Inc.*, you are showing others how well you can negotiate for them when you are on their side of the table.

- **Relax**. This is where that inner voice, or 'gut instinct', is crucial and you must be relaxed enough to hear it. When you stay relaxed, you are allowing the atmosphere to remain congenial.

Flexible Thinker Tool #5
Determining Your BATNA

BATNA refers to Best Alternative to a Negotiated Agreement. It is critical to prepare this agreement before the negotiations begin. You have to be ready to walk away from the deal if it is not right. By preparing your BATNA, you will be able to relax and negotiate from a position of strength, instead of desperation and weakness.

Here are four key steps to help you to prepare your BATNA:

1 Invent a list of actions to take if no agreement is reached.

2 Improve on some of the most promising ideas and convert them into practical alternatives.

3 Select the one alternative that seems best, and use the second best alternative as a fallback choice.

4 Consider the other party's BATNA to estimate what you can expect from the negotiation.

Write everything out. It is not good enough to simply have it in your head. You need to write it out clearly. Here is a sample BATNA worksheet. If you like, you can visit our web site at **www.flexiblethinker.com** to download a BATNA worksheet for your own use.

BATNA WORKSHEET

Expected Outcome(s) of the Negotiation

_____

_____

_____

_____

Criteria for Alternative Options

Must-Haves   Like-to-Haves

_____   _____

_____   _____

_____   _____

Your Alternatives

	Option	+ Advantages	- Disadvantages
Yours			
Theirs			

Best Alternatives   Yours   Theirs

#1 _____

#2 _____

Your fifth tool—BATNA
BATNA means *Best Alternative to a Negotiated Agreement*

Now That You Are in the Middle of Negotiating....

This is where all of your preparation begins to shine through. Because you have done your homework and are prepared, you are able to use your *Relax* tool to its best effect. Still, it is a tense situation. You are dealing with other people and there may be information you do not know. Here are some *Flexible Thinker*® tools you can apply to help in this situation.

Flexible Thinker Tool #6
Yes and Because

This is one of the most effective tools you will ever learn. It is both an amazing, assertive communication tool and a great brainstorming technique because it is so simple. *Yes* acknowledges what the person is saying. *Because* is an active listening technique for finding and/or understanding the person's justification for the idea. *And* builds on the idea by adding to it or taking it in a new direction.

Try this exercise. Sit down with another person and take your orange. The first person comes up with an idea such as, "It can be used as a lethal weapon."

That person then passes the orange to the next person who has to say, "Yes, it can be used as a lethal weapon because..." The person then gives justification for the previous person's idea (i.e. "It can be used as a lethal weapon because it is round and hard", etc.). The person then uses the phrase, "and it can also be used as a ...." and adds another function (i.e. "and it can also be used for perfume"). S/he then hands the orange to a different person who repeats the game.

You have just brainstormed with 'Yes and Because'.

Your sixth tool—*Yes and Because*

Yes and Because* means *Acknowledge and Build

Ask any person who does comedy improvisation what the most important thing is to know. S/he will tell you it is 'yes and.' This is because 'yes and' encourages both the flow of idea and relationship. We add the word 'because' to force you to be in the moment so that you can really listen and understand what the person is saying. In workshop after workshop people have told us that this tool has changed their lives. It is very easy to use and is not even necessary for the other party to understand it. You can use this tool on your partner, your friends, your kids, or at any time when you have to interact with people in a positive way.

An electrical company had a power grid in some very remote areas where there was a lot of snow. Every winter, some of these power lines would go down because of ice and snow buildup. The only place where the lines weren't going down was in areas inhabited by bears. The bears would try to climb to get food and by doing so, they would knock down the ice and the snow.

A team of engineers was asked to figure out ways to keep these lines clear in the winter. There were literally hundreds of miles of these lines that needed to be cleared. How were they going to do it? Using the 'yes and because' tool, they decided to try a little brainstorming session. The ground rules were very simple. No matter what was said, the next person had to acknowledge it (the 'yes'), find the justification for the idea (the 'because') and add to it (the 'and').

The first person was a bit mischievous and offered the idea of putting honey pots at the top of the electrical poles. The next person had to find justification for the idea. He said, "Yes, we could put honey pots at the top of the electrical poles because bears like honey and they would try to climb the poles in order to get at the honey pots on the top and by climbing the poles they would shake the poles which would vibrate the lines and knock the ice and the snow off them. 'And' if we flew helicopters low over these lines they would vibrate and knock the ice and snow off in the same way."

That was the solution to their challenge—to fly helicopters low over the electrical lines. It was, however, the crazy idea of putting honey pots on the top of the electrical poles that led to the best idea.

This is a good example of how 'yes and because' can be used to build ideas. Remember that even crazy ideas have a logic and sometimes it is those crazy ideas that lead to the best idea. However, what happens if you don't want to build new ideas with another person? You are negotiating and really believe that your position is important enough not to change. Can you still use 'yes and because'? The answer is absolutely! There are two types of flow—the flow of ideas (as in brainstorming) and the flow of relationships. Both of these are very important. Even though you may disagree with another person, you want the relationship flow to continue so that both of you can be understood. In this case, you can use 'yes and because' to actively listen to what the person is saying, and then make your point.

When Joe entered into negotiations, he knew exactly what he wanted and what he needed. He was also aware just how marketable he was at this point in his career and was determined to get exactly what was on his list of wants.

"I applied the 'yes and because' during the very important salary negotiations. The company had salary bands and could not pay me my desired base salary," Joe commented. "My reply to the human resource manager and hiring manager was, "Yes, I understand you cannot pay me the $80,000 base salary because of the salary bands and because it would upset many people in the company. What if I was given a bonus of $10,000 at the end of the year if I was able to complete the goals we set in place during the negotiation process? I would then have the base salary I need, and I would still be within your corporate salary criteria for my position."

After lengthy negotiations between the two parties, Joe was able to get two $5,000 bonuses over a period of a year. It became a win-win situation for both. Joe received the money that he felt was appropriate for his experience, and the company received Joe's knowledge and expertise without stepping outside of the corporate rules.

The key elements in any negotiation are creating options and communicating with the other side. When you are negotiating your position, you will want the other person to listen to you. Therefore, you need to listen to him or her. When you listen and understand what the other person is saying and where s/he is coming from, you have a relationship flow happening that will also allow you to create a flow of ideas.

Important point—'yes and' is NOT 'yes but'! Read this carefully. Read it several times. This is a very important statement. 'But' negates what the other person is saying. You are only pretending to listen to get your reply. 'Yes and' focuses on what will work and 'yes but' focuses on what won't work. 'But' breaks the flow. Listen to an argument some time and notice how often you hear the word 'but.' 'But you did this…', 'But you did that…' Neither person is listening to the other. But… But… But… But… After awhile it sounds like a broken record. We call it 'but-ing heads.'

Any tense negotiation is the same. If you hear the word 'but' a lot, it means that one person is not listening to what the other person is saying. If you don't care about either the flow of ideas or the flow of relationship, then you can use 'but.' If a telemarketer calls you at 6:30 p.m. as you are sitting down to dinner, you may not want to create a flow with that person. Therefore, you can use the 'but.' In a negotiation with a future client, however, you want to develop a flow of both ideas and relationship and you will need to constantly use the 'yes and because' tool.

'Yes and because' helps you to:

- Acknowledge what the other person says and explain his/her logic so that s/he knows you understand.
- Influence other people's ideas by communicating in a way that builds on what they say and does not negate their position.
- Become a martial arts communicator. Use the person's energy to take him or her in your direction as opposed to trying to stop him or her and reverse his or her direction.
- Be in the 'now'. You have to actually listen to the person in order to understand his or her logic. By being present in the 'now', you start to become aware of the process and how you are treated. This may have a large impact on your decision-making process.

'Yes and because' is more than words. If you can't say yes, you can say, "I hear what you're saying" or "I see what you mean" or "I understand where you are coming from." The words are not important. It is the attitude of 'yes and because.' Folding your arms angrily and saying, 'and' is really saying 'but.' 'Yes and because' is a tool for communicating. In fact, when you break it down, the real order is 'yes because and.' It is simply a phrase for you to keep in mind. When you do so, you will be able to turn all of those 'honey pots on electrical poles' into 'helicopters.'

Taking the Situation 'Outside-the-Box'

What happens in the negotiation if the other person is stuck in his or her box? You have listened to him or her, used 'yes and because' and s/he still seems to go back to the same position over and over again without a real reason. What do you do?

We have all heard the term thinking 'outside-the-box.' It comes from an old brainteaser where you put nine dots in three rows on a piece of paper and ask somebody to draw four lines that go through all nine dots without lifting the pen off the paper. If s/he draws the lines inside the box, there is always one dot that s/he cannot cross. Today, 'outside-the-box' means creative thinking. Some people, however, are quite comfortable with their boxes. How do you take them out of the box?

"I heard this story at a pub in Ireland over a pint of beer so in no way, shape or form can I vouch for its authenticity," says A.J. "However, it is still a good story. Back in the early 90's when times were tough, many organizations in the public sector such as hospitals were facing financial crunches. So, what is the first thing that an organization does when it faces a cash shortfall?" he asks with a smirk.

"I don't know—lay off people," I guessed.

"No," A.J. says with a full smile, "they hire one of those overpriced consultants to come in and tell them what to do. Well, this hospital in Dublin was no exception. When they were facing a budget crunch, they hired an efficiency expert to tell them where the hospital could save money. It just so happened that this expert was a real fitness fanatic. He took his bike with him everywhere. So, he drove his bike to the gate and just before he was ready to go through, the guard on duty wanted to ask him a few questions.

The guard asked him question after question until the consultant finally said to the guard, "For the past five minutes people have been coming through this gate and you have not stopped to ask them any questions. Why are you asking me so many questions?"

"Well," said the guard, "you're on a bicycle and we have to fill out our bicycle book."

"Why do you have to fill out the bicycle book?" asked the consultant.

"I don't know," the guard confessed. "I've been here 15 years and we have always had to fill out the bicycle book."

"Okay," said the consultant. "Let me ask your supervisor."

When questioned, the guard's supervisor informed the consultant that he didn't know why they had a bicycle book but in the 20 years that he had worked there, they had always had to fill it out. The consultant later had a meeting with the president of the hospital and asked him about the bicycle book. "What bicycle book?" asked the president. "We don't have a bicycle book around here!"

The consultant then went back to the supervisor and asked him who might know about the bicycle book. "You can ask Old Joe," he said. "He worked here for almost 40 years until he retired a couple of years ago. He used to be my supervisor. He still lives in the area. Here's his number."

So, the consultant called Old Joe and asked him about the bicycle book. "They're still filling that thing out?!?" asked Old Joe incredulously. "That thing was implemented during World War II. As part of the war effort, gas was rationed and the doctors who could afford cars were saving their gasoline rations for the weekend to spend with their families. So many people were taking bicycles to work that the shed we had to park them in couldn't fit them all and many of the doctors were forced to park their bikes outside. Well you know the weather around here, it rains constantly. Many of the doctors were forced to ride home on wet bicycles. They got so upset that they went to the hospital administration and demanded that they build a bigger bicycle shed. So we instituted the bicycle book to figure out how big to build the bicycle shed."

Well, 50 years has gone by, the war's over, they are no longer rationing gasoline and they never built the bicycle shed but they are still filling out the bicycle book!

'What if?' also means to ask **'why'** or **'how.'** Remember, the idea is to question. If you don't understand, ask 'why' and then you can express a 'what if?'

Flexible Thinker Tool #7
What if?

What bicycle books are there in your career? What happens when you have to deal with the bicycle books of other people in a negotiation? Ask the question 'what if?' The key part of that phrase is the question mark. Question! Construct 'what if?' scenarios such as, "Yes, I understand that you're limited by classification for the salary of this position. What if we had a review in six months instead of one year instead?" Or, "What if we added an extra week of vacation time?" When you question, you provide options and take people out of their boxes.

'What if?' is not simply a tool for going 'outside-the-box', it is also an important way to understand the box. As the consultant in the story illustrates, it is critical to understand the box and the reason it is there in order to go outside of it. It is the same with negotiating. To simply 'go outside-the-box' for no reason can be an exercise in futility. By questioning, you are able to understand the box and then take both others and yourself outside of it. It gives everybody permission to think in new ways and helps you find the 'win-win' in a situation.

Your seventh tool—*What if?*

What if?* means *Question

This is an excellent tool to use in conjunction with '*yes and because.*' By acknowledging what the other person is saying, you are actively listening to him or her and creating that flow of both relationship and ideas. Then, by adding '*what if?*' to the '*yes and because*' you can probe his or her position to more fully understand it, or take that person out of his or her box in a way that keeps the relationship going while you explore the situation from many different angles.

Using All of Your Tools to Help You Negotiate

Here is a review of how you can put all of your tools together to help maximize your negotiating potential in a new opportunity.

- **Relax.** Walk away and reflect on the offers. YOU DON'T HAVE TO SAY 'YES' OR 'NO' RIGHT AWAY! Get in touch with your gut instinct and go with it. There is no deal you cannot walk away from!

- **I Want.** Decide what you want and what they want and strategize on how you can each get what you want.

- **Orange.** If the company only pays a certain salary, can you redefine part of the difference as a *signing bonus,* or can you move the review process from 12 months to four months so that it is a raise, or build in performance bonuses?

- **Library.** Do your research on the company and the industry. Try to understand as much as you can about their needs **before you walk into the interview**. The more you know, the more flexible you can be!

- **Yes and Because.** Listen to what they are saying, acknowledge their reality and then add to it.

- **What if?** Question them to understand where they are coming from, and help them to create some options together.

- **Navigate and negotiate.** Use your tools to understand this company's limitations and whether it is right for you.

Now go through your obstacles a final time. What ideas or tools can you use from this chapter to overcome obstacles you have listed that are hindering your career? How will you use these tools and ideas in your action plan?

Chapter Eight:

Six Simple Steps to a Continuous Career Management Action Plan

*"You will never 'find' time for anything.
If you want time, you must make it."*

- CHARLES BUXTON

The majority of career books and outplacement programs focus on how to get your next job. Our approach, however, is to teach people how to manage their careers and stay employed regardless of the economy. This means you need to be prepared for the eventuality of movement at all times. Our belief is that individuals are solely responsible for their careers, not the organization.

Much of the following information is a review of what you have already read in this book. The information below is an easily accessible reminder of what needs to happen to help you move forward and manage your career. The Career Search Action Plan should always be looked at as a reminder of the relationships you need to build and maintain and the actions you need to implement when participating in a job search. The Six Steps are a vital part of continuous career management and are as vital as updating your hard skills. These steps are a checkpoint review of how well you are doing at controlling and managing your career.

Career Search Action Plan

The following is an action marketing campaign that needs to be implemented for maximum results when searching for your next position.

Internet

- Post your resumé on as many job sites that have value to the type of position you are searching for as possible.
- Remember to keep track of where your resumé is posted and what types of positions you requested.
- WARNING—Individuals who spend all their time on the Internet risk becoming islands unto themselves, sending out a message in a bottle that may never be answered.
- The Internet represents only 5 percent of the positions available, so do not risk spending 80 percent of your time in a place that produces only 5 percent of the results.

Recruiters

- Seek out recruiters that specialize in your area of expertise (see Six Simple Steps).

- Start by applying to as many recruiters as possible, and then narrow them down to a select few.
- Recruiters hold 25 percent to 30 percent of the positions available (see Six Simple Steps).

Target Marketing

Target Marketing Techniques

The following is a list of creative ways to target market specific companies and industries.

Put your feet up on the desk and read the newspaper.
- Read the newspaper and business magazines every day.
- Target companies that are featured in articles.
- Send a handwritten note or make a phone call to the person featured in the article telling him or her how much you enjoyed the information.
- Send a handwritten note or make a phone call to the individuals who have just been promoted congratulating them.
- Research and watch out for industries that are in a growth mode.

Networking
- Sixty percent+ of available jobs are hidden and can only be discovered by networking.
- The old adage, 'it's not what you know but who you know' is still very true in today's market (see Six Simple Steps).

How to implement and manage your time and marketing campaign when searching for a job:

- Spend a minimum of four hours per day on your marketing campaign (or one hour if you are working).
- Pick the technique you like the least and do it at the beginning of your day (i.e. if you hate networking and love the Internet, start with networking and finish with the Internet).

- The stat rule for the average sales campaign is that for every 100 brochures sent out, it takes 100 follow-up calls to create 10 appointments to lead to one sale. Replace the brochure with your resumé and the numbers necessary to reach the goal of landing a position can be even higher.

- It is crucial to work all four areas simultaneously for maximum results. You cannot market and sell any product by simply placing an ad in the newspaper (and that is basically what the Internet is for the 21st century). You need to market the product in many different ways to make sure it is noticed in as many venues as possible.

- By working all four areas at once you will create the synergy and numbers you need to start getting interviews and eventually an offer. If you are still employed, you may have to break up the areas, or do the work on different days. You can use vacation days, lunch hours, evenings and weekends. Remember, your work supports every aspect of your life.

Six Simple Steps to Continuous Career Management

The following six steps can be implemented as part of your career maintenance program to help you move easily and effortlessly from one position to another. Preparation is the vehicle that will keep you employed, not a corporation.

Step One—Be a Strategic Career Planner

- Get the '*Me Inc.*' attitude—know that you are the one responsible for your career and your next career move.

- Don't fool yourself into thinking that you are indispensable to any corporation.

- In the 21st century, everyone should be a knowledge worker, therefore, you must remember that you are the sum total of all your career experiences. Knowledge is what you are selling to a potential client/employer.

- Transferable skills are the lifeline to career stability.

- Develop transferable skills through continued training and education even if that means paying for the training yourself.
- Hard skills may get the position but soft skills keep the opportunities growing.
- Understand bottom line accountability and what that means to the corporation you presently work for.

Step Two—Keep an Accomplishment Journal

Everyone gets a job description of duties, responsibilities and expectations. What you accomplish within those guidelines is what will set you apart from other people in the corporate world and in the workplace.

The number one style of interviewing is the behavioral interview and to be successful you must be able to articulate and give examples of your accomplishments, how you solved problems, met deadlines and improved systems and processes, etc.

This information should be tracked on a regular basis and used to update your resumé. The following are examples of specifics you should be tracking:

- Developed continuous process improvements within billing production, resulting in invoices being delivered to customers in an accurate and timely fashion.
- Managed the implementation of projects including system enhancement and process re-engineering, which improved company results and objectives for the year 2001.
- Co-coordinated the logistics of building new telecommunications systems for six new office sites across Canada within four months—'on cost' and 'on time.'
- Reorganized the filing system to ensure easy access to corporate documents.
- Increased sales by 20 percent by implementing a national sales and marketing campaign
- Created a marketing plan that increased sales by 20 percent.

- Devised action plans to resolve a myriad of tricky situations and bring teams of people together to carry out these plans, ensuring continued customer satisfaction.

- Reduced receivables from 48 to 32 days by creating and implementing a new follow-up process

- Successfully co-coordinated and managed the administration and report production of 28 sales representatives.

The trick is to review this every quarter. If you find yourself time and time again not having any accomplishments to speak of, ask some tough questions such as:

- Is my present position allowing me the opportunity to gain the experience and knowledge I need to keep my career on the move and be prepared for the future?

- Will I be able to answer behavioral type questions during the interview process?

- Is my career standing still? Am I just doing my job and filling in time?

If you are not learning new skills, gaining knowledge and keeping up with new technology, process and systems, you may be committing career suicide and have to pay the price when you start to look for your next position.

Step Three—The Power of a Resumé

Walk around with a resumé in your back pocket at all times.

Not having a resumé is the number one reason people feel they are stuck in a job/position. The number one reason for not having a resumé is, "I don't have the time to write one." In this market you can't afford not to have one.

How would it feel to have a resumé that is up-to-date and successfully speaks to your accomplishments?

Investigate the current styles and trends for resumé writing.

The look of a resumé can date you immediately. Nothing says, 'behind the times' more than an old-fashioned resumé format. It can also say you have not even bothered to keep up with the market trends. A resumé is a work in progress, not something you dust off every few years to add your latest experiences.

The best way to keep track of current resumé trends is to head to the bookstore or library. There are hundreds of books on this subject; however I suggest you find a book that relates to the Canadian market. Recruiters are also a great source of information and can give you some pointers.

The following is a list of some of the latest market information on resumé writing:

1. Two pages are all that is required.
2. Check for spelling and grammar—have two friends check your resumé, as well.
3. Do not include outdated information—most HR professionals and recruiters do not want to look at information that is more than 10 years old.
4. Education should be at the end of the resumé, not the beginning.
5. Resumés should clearly state your achievements and accomplishments combined with a brief outline of responsibilities.
6. Hard skills such as up-to-date technical and computers skills should be showcased on your resumé.

Apply for a position at least once a year.

No matter how secure you think your present position is, would it not be comforting to know just how marketable you really are?

It is not disloyal to your present employer to keep an eye on your marketability. It is savvy career management.

When you are employed is a great time to find out if you are actually marketable. What would happen if you sent your resumé out to recruiters and posted your resumé on the Internet and you got no response? If you receive no response, ask the following questions and take the action necessary:

- Are my skills, education, knowledge and experiences in line with what employers are looking for?
- Is my resumé capturing and marketing my skills and accomplishments in a current and proper format?
- Do I have current hard skills—systems, processes, computer and technical skills?

A resumé is the tool that gives you the power to move forward in the 21st century workforce.

Step Four—Understanding the Marketplace

A number of years ago, a friend came to me with a career decision he had to make. He felt it was time to look at his industry and where it was going. John was a sales manager and had been with his company for 10 years. He had received a number of promotions and had been the recipient of many awards. In the last two years he had noticed that business was slowing down significantly.

John had been offered a position with a start-up company by the former president of his current company. His fear was that he would lose well-established credibility and have to start over developing a whole new market. At the same time, he was concerned about the direction his present industry was heading in.

John was advised to research the marketplace, its current trends, and take the time to investigate by reading newspapers, business magazines and books. In addition, he was told to speak and network with everyone he knew and ask questions.

After a month of research John took the new opportunity. His old company supplied cheques to banks and financial institutes. The new company supplied automatic teller machines to retail stores, gas stations and restaurants.

Understanding the marketplace is crucial to your career survival. Your current industry competitor today can be your employer tomorrow.

- Spend at least one to two hours per week researching and reading about your marketplace.

Step Five—Partner with Recruiters throughout the Lifetime of your Career

Regardless of your past experiences with recruiters, the facts speak for themselves.

- The recruitment industry is a multi-billion-dollar industry.
- The number one staffing service did $18 billion in sales in 2002.
- Every one of the Fortune 100 companies used staffing services in the year 2001.
- According to *Free Agent Nation* by Daniel Pink, the top employer in 2001 was Manpower, not Ford or GM.
- Thirty-eight percent of all contract/temporary positions become full-time according to Statistics Canada.

If the above information is not enough to compel you to seek out a recruiter, how about the fact that 25 to 30 percent of all positions are in the hands of recruiters. Only 5 to 10 percent of positions come from the Internet. Yet 80 percent of a job seeker's time is spent on the Internet looking for work.

Finding the right recruiter that specializes in your industry is not easy. A recruiter's role is not to find jobs for people, but to fill positions for their paying clients.

People always ask for the names of good recruiters and staffing services. Like any professional service, there are good and bad. It is up to you to seek out recruiters and develop the relationship. The foundation to a good relationship or partnership is built over time. The following is a list of the most successful ways to attract a recruiter's attention.

- Recruiter's directory
- Persistence/Follow-up
- Sharing industry knowledge and exchanging information with a recruiter
- Referrals
- Associations

Recruiters are also a great source of industry information. Because of their relationships with companies, they always have their fingers on the pulse of the marketplace. They know who is hiring, where the latest trends are, as well as the markets that are not doing well.

Step Six—Networking is the Key to Survival and Career Success

Recruiters may hold 25 to 30 percent of the jobs, but networking creates 60 to 70 percent of all positions. This is a skill you must develop.

Think about the individual who may not necessarily have the best skills or be the brightest, but always takes the time to speak with management and other people in the company. Now think about the individual who gets the job done, is always on top of his or her skills and work, but is too busy to bother with what goes on in the office. Who gets the promotion?

Networking is about exchanging information, not asking for a job.

Networking is about developing a core group of people who you can help and who can also help you along your career path.

Networking is about investing in future possibilities.

Networking is an art and one that requires time and effort. The following are some of the ways that you can expand and increase your networking skills:

- Attend workshops and training sessions on networking. Don't forget to keep a list of the names of everyone in the session.
- Write down the name of everyone you know and take the time to keep in touch. E-mail is a great time saver.
- Join networking groups.
- Become a member of industry associations.
- Volunteer.
- Phone people you previously worked with just to say hi.

- Help people along the way—the individual who is great at networking is always willing to give out more information then s/he will ever receive.

The Personal Coach

Throughout this book we have asked you to answer questions and advised you to take an honest look at your career and how to move it forward. We would like to leave you with some powerful career questions that you can spend time asking yourself. This will help you create a benchmark of where you are and what needs to happen to help you achieve your career goals. We hope that by questioning yourself on an ongoing basis, you will challenge your beliefs and create a career that fulfills your potential. It is our goal to give you the tools to take control of your career. These questions can also help you determine if you are involved in your career, or are just 'ghosting.'

The following group of questions was created by career coach Deborah Bakti:

Why it's important to ask questions....

- Questions are like spark plugs for our brains—they stimulate thinking, reflection, creativity.
- The quality of the question directly impacts the quality of the answer. For example, asking, "Why am I stuck in this dead-end job?" is going to give you some pretty pathetic answers. However, asking yourself questions like, "What do I need to do differently to work in the ideal job? What limiting choices have I made? What limiting beliefs have I bought into? What opportunities am I not taking? What risks am I afraid of taking? What am I avoiding?" allow more room to really think about what's going on, what needs to change, what you need to do differently. They are empowering questions that provide insight and will lead to action.

Here are some other questions to consider:
What do I expect to learn/develop/achieve at the end of three months/six months/one year?

- How will I know I have achieved this?
- How will I measure success?
- What actions do I need to take?
- What could get in my way?
- What help do I need to achieve this?
- How will I be accountable to get this support?
- What am I committed to?
- What do I want?

The 'What do I want?' is the toughest question. It is our belief that many people don't think enough about their 'I Want.' This means that they are likely to miss an opportunity that may be right in front of them. Remember that it is never too late to take control of your career. We would like to leave you with these words:

In order to move forward, you must focus on future visions and not past grievances.

It is in that future vision that the career you deserve lies. It is in that future that you will achieve the highest performance for both yourself and the clients/organizations that utilize your talents.

Extreme Performance

A Measurable Approach to Maximizing Productivity
A Flexible Thinker® Approach

This interactive program is designed to provide you with the tools to create accomplishments that have a bottom line effect on the organization. These tools will help you become a more engaged and productive performer. Through the use of the Accomplishment Journal™ and the C.A.R.™ technique, the organization will be able to measure the effect of this program on the bottom line and in performance reviews.

Come and Learn:

- Tools that allow employees to think in new ways about their career within the organization and how to tie-in organizational performance to personal goals.
- How to redefine the employer employee relationship in a way that benefits both.
- Create a corporate environment where "ghosting" & "the water cooler syndrome" does not exist.
- New approaches to being flexible under change and generate opportunities to problems under pressure.
- How to apply these tools to help others develop their own "I Want" and measure their achievements.
- How to motivate others when there are changes happening within the organization or team that are affecting morale.

For more information on this workshop, contact us at info@flexiblethinker.com

Continuous Career Management:

The Revolutionary Approach that Empowers You to Own Your Career
A Flexible Thinker® Approach

Are you managing your career or focusing on lack of employer-employee loyalty? This workshop will give you the tools to take control of your career by incorporating creative problem solving tools with traditional job aids to change the way you think and approach your career.

Come and Learn:

- How to shift career management from the organization to you.

- Tools that allow you to think in new ways about their career.

- How to redefine the employer employee relationship in a way that benefits both.

- Create a corporate environment where "ghosting" & "the water cooler syndrome" does not exist.

- New approaches to being flexible under change and generate opportunities to problems under pressure.

- How to maximize your investment in your career by giving you the tools to face your situation in new ways.

- How to prepare yourself for the future regardless of the economy.

For more information on this workshop, contact us at info@flexiblethinker.com

About the authors

MICHAEL ROSENBERG is the author of *The Flexible Thinker®: A Guide to Creative Wealth*. He has worked with numerous organizations across North America to solve problems. His program has been used by one municipality to build a million dollar life safety center with no tax payer dollars, help solve an engine design problem for a large manufacturer, and tripled sales and quadrupled profitability for a small company with a $2,000 marketing budget. Michael has lectured on accelerated learning design and given talks at numerous universities. *The Flexible Thinker®* program has been studied extensively by the University of Western Ontario's Ivey School of Business and found to have a significant impact within the organization. Mike is also the founder of both Leadership Peel, a grassroots organization that helps build community leadership for the western suburbs of Toronto. He is also the artistic director of the *R9 Comedy Troupe*.

SANDRA BOYD is the author of *The Hidden Job Market*. Sandra has been widely published and quoted across the U.S. and Canada in such publications as the Globe and Mail to discuss the paradigm shift in the workplace. In addition to providing career transition and career coaching to clients at management, professional and administrative levels, Sandra also facilitates various workshops and career transition programs for a wide variety of public and private sector organizations. These workshops include *Networking, Negotiations, Behavioral Interviewing,* and her original program "Six Simple Steps to Continuous Career Management".

Index

Other Flexible Thinker® Guide to Books:

The Flexible Thinker: A Guide to Creative Wealth

Upcoming Flexible Thinker® Guide to Books:

The Flexible Leader

Sales Tools for the Real World

Effective and Assertive Communication

Dealing with Stress